MW00616361

MATH HACKS FOR SCRATCH®

Unlock the Power of Math with Scratch Programming

by Michael Mays

no starch press®

San Francisco

MATH HACKS FOR SCRATCH®. Copyright © 2025 by Michael Mays.

All rights reserved. No part of this work may be reproduced or transmitted in any form or by any means, electronic or mechanical, including photocopying, recording, or by any information storage or retrieval system, without the prior written permission of the copyright owner and the publisher.

Printed in China

First printing

28 27 26 25 24   1 2 3 4 5

ISBN-13: 978-1-7185-0338-0 (print)
ISBN-13: 978-1-7185-0339-7 (ebook)

Published by No Starch Press®, Inc.
245 8th Street, San Francisco, CA 94103
phone: +1.415.863.9900
www.nostarch.com; info@nostarch.com

Publisher: William Pollock
Managing Editor: Jill Franklin
Production Manager: Sabrina Plomitallo-González
Production Editor: Miles Bond
Developmental Editor: Nathan Heidelberger
Cover Illustrator: Gina Redman
Technical Reviewer: Peter Farrell
Copyeditor: Rachel Head
Proofreader: Scout Festa

Library of Congress Control Number: 2024012817

For customer service inquiries, please contact info@nostarch.com. For information on distribution, bulk sales, corporate sales, or translations: sales@nostarch.com. For permission to translate this work: rights@nostarch.com. To report counterfeit copies or piracy: counterfeit@nostarch.com.

The information in this book is distributed on an "As Is" basis, without warranty. While every precaution has been taken in the preparation of this work, neither the author nor No Starch Press, Inc. shall have any liability to any person or entity with respect to any loss or damage caused or alleged to be caused directly or indirectly by the information contained in it.

Trademark Notice

No Starch Press and the No Starch Press iron logo are registered trademarks of No Starch Press, Inc. Other product and company names mentioned herein may be the trademarks of their respective owners. Rather than use a trademark symbol with every occurrence of a trademarked name, we are using the names only in an editorial fashion and to the benefit of the trademark owner, with no intention of infringement of the trademark.

The Scratch name, Scratch logo, and Scratch Cat are trademarks owned by the Scratch Team. Screenshots in this book are licensed under the Creative Commons Attribution-ShareAlike 2.0 license. Scratch is developed by the Lifelong Kindergarten Group at the MIT Media Lab. See *http://scratch.mit.edu*.

To Conor, Nora, and Clara, three supergenius kittens

About the Author

Michael Mays is a professor emeritus of the Eberly College of Arts and Sciences at West Virginia University, where he taught for 40 years. During his tenure, he also served as director of the Institute for Math Learning and chair of the Department of Statistics. He's had research appointments at the University of Queensland in Brisbane, Australia, and the University of the Witwatersrand in Johannesburg, South Africa. Michael has written 62 research papers and technical reports on number theory, combinatorics, and mathematics education.

About the Technical Reviewer

Peter Farrell has taught math and computer science for over 15 years and is dedicated to helping people of all ages learn math and programming. In 2019, his second book, *Math Adventures with Python*, was published by No Starch Press. He lives in North Texas.

BRIEF CONTENTS

CONTENTS IN DETAIL

6

MAKING CODES, AND CRACKING THEM TOO   101

7

EXPERIMENTS IN COUNTING   129

8

THREE HELPINGS OF PI   151

Acknowledgments

I've learned from many people who used computers to explore ideas in mathematics classrooms. My first microcomputer number theory labs were written on an Osborne I using muMATH, a computer algebra system developed by Albert D. Rich and David Stoutemyer in the late 1970s. Thanks to Hugh Montgomery, whose *Computational Laboratories in Number Theory (CLINT)*, written using Turbo Pascal, inspired computer explorations in many of my classes over the years, and to Joe Yanik, whose Math Toolkit for Java Developers let me build many online activities for students in college algebra, trigonometry, and calculus. Thanks to Nicholas Jackiw and *The Geometer's Sketchpad*®, which brought dynamic geometry to life. Thanks to Conor Mays for many useful tips about Scratch and much encouragement, and for his comments on an early version of this book.

Special thanks to my editor, Nathan Heidelberger, whose careful scrutiny and wise suggestions kept the book focused on its audience at all times. I appreciate Bill Pollock, big fish at No Starch Press, for giving the book a chance, and the NSP team for bringing it to completion and to market.

Introduction

This book uses Scratch to invite exploration with math. It presents concepts such as number representations, divisibility, prime numbers, and cryptography that are useful and relevant in daily life and that are fun to code. It's about how to ask interesting mathematical questions and how to program a computer to answer them.

The book is also about finding the best way to solve a problem. You'll see how a little bit of planning, combined with the right mathematical or coding tricks, can make complex calculations doable. These are the "hacks" in the book's title; you'll learn programming strategies for coaxing Scratch into giving you the answer you want and mathematical tricks that offer neat solutions to seemingly impossible problems.

Why Scratch?

Exploring a computer language involves seeing what it can do and figuring out how it can answer the questions you want to ask. Scratch is a language that encourages play. While it's often used to create graphics, sound, and games, its spirit of play works for exploring math, too.

Scratch is simple to use: it runs directly in a web browser through the Scratch website, *https://scratch.mit.edu*, with no installation required (although you can download the Scratch app from *https://scratch.mit.edu/download* if you'd prefer to work offline). You create programs by putting commands together like LEGO® bricks, with all the options immediately available via drag-and-drop. The block-based interface lets you focus on combining loops, conditionals, and variables to build whatever you want, without getting bogged down in the syntax details of a text-based language. If you've used Scratch to make games or write stories, it's easy to start using it to answer math-related questions.

Who This Book Is For

This book is for you if:

* You like Scratch programming and want to learn more about it
* You like math and are ready to see some new ideas
* You like puzzles and patterns
* You know how good it feels when you find the best way to solve a problem

You'll get the most out of this book if you have some basic Scratch programming experience already. For example, you should be comfortable creating your own variables, lists, and custom blocks. It will also help to have some knowledge of algebra and geometry, such as understanding how to work with algebraic variables and interpret points on a coordinate plane. You'll be amazed by what you can do in Scratch with just these few ingredients, from finding all the prime numbers in a set to creating unbreakable secret codes.

What's in This Book

Here's an overview of what you'll find in each chapter of the book:

Chapter 1: What Computers Think About Numbers We'll start by exploring how computers keep track of numbers internally. Knowing this can help you avoid tricky errors and overcome some of the limits of a programming language.

Chapter 2: Exploring Divisibility and Primes Next, we'll investigate prime numbers, which are the building blocks of all integers. You'll see how Scratch can help you find prime numbers and use them for computations.

Chapter 3: Splitting Numbers with Prime Factorization This chapter presents different strategies for figuring out how to write a number as a product of primes. Testing out different techniques will help you find the most efficient strategy.

Chapter 4: Finding Patterns in Sequences In this chapter, you'll learn how to use Scratch to make sense of patterns in lists of numbers. Sometimes the patterns come from algebra, sometimes from geometry, and sometimes both.

Chapter 5: From Sequences to Arrays   Having mastered one-dimensional lists, we'll move on to two-dimensional tables of numbers, like multiplication tables and Pascal's triangle. You'll learn strategies for keeping track of two-dimensional data structures in Scratch.

Chapter 6: Making Codes, and Cracking Them Too   This chapter will show you how to use mathematical rules to scramble messages into gibberish. You'll also discover techniques for unscrambling those messages, with or without a secret key.

Chapter 7: Experiments in Counting   Next, we'll tackle two interesting problems from the field of combinatorics, also called the art of counting. You'll see how Scratch can make patterns out of simple rules and count how many ways the patterns can occur.

Chapter 8: Three Helpings of Pi   In this chapter, you'll try out different ways of calculating the value of π, including by area, by convergence, and by using number theory.

Chapter 9: What Next?   The final chapter offers some suggestions about where to look for more math and programming problems and for more tools to solve them.

Every chapter features a series of hands-on Scratch coding projects so you can see the chapter's concepts in action. There are 33 projects in all. Challenges throughout the book will also help you build on the ideas and programs discussed in each chapter. The book's appendix contains some sample code and hints on how to approach these challenges.

How to Read This Book

The easiest way to read this book is like a novel, straight through from beginning to end. The topics covered are largely independent, though, so you can read the chapters out of order if you like. If you're particularly interested in one of the chapter topics, you might want to skip ahead to that one; or maybe one of the chapters is relevant to a subject you're studying in school and you'd like to start there. Exploring in this way is absolutely fine, but I do have a couple of recommendations.

Chapter 1, about computer arithmetic, will help you understand what can go wrong with arithmetic in the programs in later chapters. It's a good idea to read this one first. Chapter 2 introduces prime numbers, so you should read it before Chapter 3, which builds prime factorizations. You'll probably also want to read Chapter 4, on sequences, before Chapter 5, on arrays, since arrays can be thought of as the two-dimensional equivalent of one-dimensional sequences. The following chapters all stand alone, but Chapter 7, in particular, goes into some pretty complex concepts and programs; working through some of the other chapters before you tackle that one might be a good idea in order to get more practice with Scratch programming and mathematical thinking.

Online Resources

You can find the Scratch code for all 33 projects and most of the challenge problems online at the Scratch studio for this book, *https://scratch.mit.edu/studios/29153814*. The programs are also available for download from this book's web page at *https://nostarch.com/math-hacks-scratch*.

My Inspiration

I wrote this book with my grandchildren in mind. When they introduced me to Scratch, I was immediately struck by the language's mascot, that smiling ginger kitten. I didn't know the mascot's name, but it might as well have been Gummitch, the precocious main character in one of my favorite short stories, "Space-Time for Springers" by Fritz Leiber. Gummitch is a supergenius kitten who has big plans to write books explaining the world to other supergenius kittens, including *The Encyclopedia of Odors*, *Anthropofeline Psychology*, and, most intriguing of all, *Space-Time for Springers*.

Seeing Scratch Cat's resemblance to Gummitch, I wanted to write the math book Gummitch would have written, a sort of *Numbers for Springers*. I've aimed to keep the mathematical level of the book just right for supergenius kittens everywhere. The book's projects were fun to write and fun to hack in Scratch, combining a little bit of math with Scratch code to open up new ways to think about numbers, letters, geometry, and patterns. I hope you'll enjoy the reading as much as I enjoyed the writing!

1

What Computers Think About Numbers

 To do math, a computer needs a way of representing numbers. As it turns out, computers think about numbers pretty differently than humans do.

For example, we like to think we can keep counting to higher and higher numbers forever, but computers have a limited amount of storage space. If they start counting, they eventually run out of room. There is no biggest number, but there *is* a biggest number your computer can represent in Scratch.

Similarly, we think about fractions and decimal numbers as matching up with points on a number line, with an infinite number of points fitting between any two whole numbers. But as we pack points more and more tightly together in the finite world of computers, eventually we run out of room to keep track of them. There is no smallest positive number, but there *is* a smallest positive number your computer can work with in Scratch.

In this chapter, we'll look at what's going on behind your computer screen and how computers think about numbers. We'll explore the limitations of what numbers Scratch can represent. It's important to understand these limits so we can be sure the results we get from a program are accurate. You'll also learn some hacks for getting around Scratch's limits and tricking the computer into representing more numbers than would normally be possible.

What Are Numbers, Anyway?

Everybody *thinks* they know what numbers are, but there are many number systems to choose from, depending on what we want the numbers to do. We usually learn to count with numbers starting from 1, so we call those numbers *counting numbers*. Sometimes we want to start counting from 0, in which case the numbers are called *whole numbers*. When we go forward and backward, allowing negative numbers too, we generate the set of *integers*: {..., –3, –2, –1, 0, 1, 2, 3, ...}.

We can make an association with geometry and think of numbers as corresponding to points on a line, building the set of *real numbers*. We can also divide integers by other (nonzero) integers to make *rational numbers*. Here we use *rational* not to mean logical and making sense, but because the numbers are built from *ratios*. Sometimes rational numbers are called *fractions*, but this can be misleading. In common language, a *fraction* of something is only a portion of it, suggesting a part less than 1, whereas rational numbers like 3/2 and 4/3 can be bigger than 1. Also, fractions are usually thought of with a denominator of 2 or more (halves, thirds, and so on), but rational numbers sometimes have a denominator of 1, as in 2/1, 3/1, and so on. In this way, an integer is a special kind of rational number.

With all these kinds of numbers, we use our intuition that when we name a particular number, we're identifying one element of an infinite collection. That is, we expect numbers to go on forever: "To infinity and beyond," as Buzz Lightyear says. There's another way that numbers can be used, though, where they wrap around and recycle their values over and over, like the numbers on a clock. This way of working with numbers is useful for tracking things that happen regularly or repeatedly, and it has some interesting properties that we'll explore in the next chapter when we look at modular arithmetic.

In the first few chapters of this book, we'll be most interested in counting numbers, also called *positive integers*. When we talk about numbers without being more specific, that's the default interpretation to use. But so far, we've considered only what numbers are or aren't included in a number system. There's a whole other factor to consider as well: how those numbers are *represented*.

Base 10? Base 2? You Pick!

A *basis representation system* determines how numbers are broken down into groups for ease of counting and how many symbols are needed to represent those numbers. Probably because we have 10 fingers, humans typically think of numbers in *decimal*, a basis system that uses groups of 10. We start counting one at a time and use a different symbol for each new number, 1 through 9. When we run out of fingers, we group double handfuls of fingers and count by tens. When there are no units left over after separating groups of 10, we use the symbol 0, a closed fist, to show this. So we understand 34 as 3 tens and 4 ones, and 60 as 6 tens and 0 ones.

We can extend the pattern of grouping by 10 to represent increasingly large numbers with relatively few digits, introducing a third-place digit for 10 tens (100), a fourth place for 10 hundreds (1,000), and so on. It helps to use exponents to indicate the repeated multiplication. For example:

$$10^2 = 10 \cdot 10 = 100$$
$$10^3 = 10 \cdot 10 \cdot 10 = 10 \cdot 100 = 1,000$$
$$\cdots$$

We always have the option of sorting out the grouping using expanded notation. Here's an example:

$$35,062 = (3 \cdot 10^4) + (5 \cdot 10^3) + (0 \cdot 10^2) + (6 \cdot 10^1) + (2 \cdot 10^0)$$

Since the decimal system hinges on powers of 10, it's also called *base 10*. But while humans favor base 10, other ways of grouping are possible. For example, if you wanted to count using only the fingers on one hand, you could group by fives and have a *base 5* system. Base 5 numeration needs only the symbols 0, 1, 2, 3, and 4. The number five is written as 10, six as 11, and so on.

Eggs and donuts are sold by the dozen, a group of 12, and we even have a word for a dozen dozen: a *gross*. *Base 12* numeration uses the symbols 0, 1, 2, 3, 4, 5, 6, 7, 8, and 9 as usual, but it needs two extra single-digit symbols to represent the numbers ten and eleven. Usually we use T and E. If we need to specify the base, we can do it with a subscript, such as 15_{10} to indicate that 15 is written in base 10. This makes it easier to compare numbers written in different basis systems. For example, $15_{10} = 13_{12} = 30_5$, which is to say that $(1 \cdot 10) + 5 = (1 \cdot 12) + 3 = (3 \cdot 5) + 0$.

Most computers use a *base 2* system, also called *binary*, to represent numbers internally. This system has the advantage that it requires only two symbols, 0 and 1. This matters because 0 and 1 are easy to keep track of with the position of a switch: the switch is either off (0) or on (1). Having only two symbols is good for expressing logic, too, where the two possibilities could represent *false* and *true*. A drawback is that powers of 2 (1, 2, 4, 8, 16, ...) grow more slowly than powers of 10 (1, 10, 100, 1,000, ...), so it typically takes more digits to represent a number in binary than it does to represent the same number in decimal. We'll talk more about this later.

Project 1: What's 77 in Binary?

For a given positive integer, there's a unique way of writing it in base 10, and it also has a unique representation in binary. In this project, we'll write a Scratch program that converts from decimal to binary so we can see what the computer is seeing when it represents a number.

There are two ways we might approach this problem: strategies we can call *big-to-little* and *little-to-big*. According to the big-to-little strategy, we first find the largest power of 2 contained in a decimal number, to determine the leftmost digit of the base 2 representation. Then we subtract that power of 2 and find the largest power of 2 in the difference. We keep repeating this process to build up the binary representation, generating the digits from left to right. For example:

$$77_{10} = 64 + 13$$
$$= 64 + 8 + 5$$
$$= 64 + 8 + 4 + 1$$
$$= 2^6 + 2^3 + 2^2 + 1$$
$$= (1 \cdot 2^6) + (0 \cdot 2^5) + (0 \cdot 2^4) + (1 \cdot 2^3) + (1 \cdot 2^2) + (0 \cdot 2^1) + 1$$
$$= 1001101_2$$

The big-to-little strategy matches the way most humans would approach doing a decimal-to-binary conversion in their heads, but the little-to-big strategy is much easier to code on a computer. Instead of searching for the largest power of 2 contained in a number, all we have to do is program a series of divisions by 2 and keep track of the remainders. This builds up the binary representation from right to left. Figure 1-1 shows a Scratch program that uses the little-to-big approach.

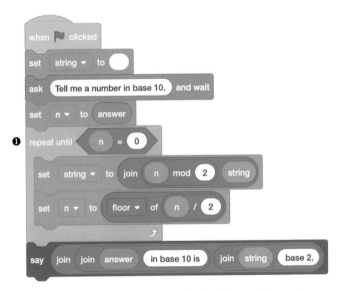

Figure 1-1: A program to convert decimal (base 10) numbers into binary (base 2)

We build up the binary version of a number in the string variable, which starts out blank at the beginning of the program. (A *string* is a sequence of characters; more on this in "Hacking the Code" on page 5.) To get started, we use the ask and wait block to have Scratch Cat prompt the user for a number in base 10, storing the user's answer in the n variable. Then we enter a repeat until loop ❶, where the real logic is.

n mod 2 returns the remainder of dividing n by 2, which will be 1 if n is odd or 0 if n is even. Each time through the loop, this mod operation gives us one digit of the binary representation of the number, starting with the least significant (rightmost) digit. We use the join block to merge that digit with the contents already in the string variable, putting the result back in string. Then we divide n by 2 and use floor to round the result down to the nearest whole number. This removes the value of the binary digit we just accounted for from n. Then, the loop can start again to find the next binary digit.

Once n gets down to 0, we've built up the complete binary representation of the number from right to left. We then use some more join blocks to put together a meaningful sentence reporting the result, which Scratch Cat announces through the say block.

The Results

Run the program and try entering **77** when Scratch Cat asks for a number. You should get 1001101 as the result, as shown in Figure 1-2.

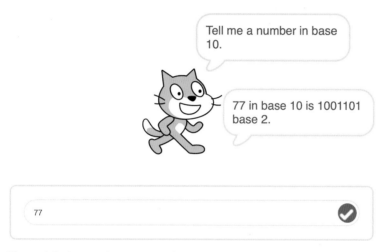

Tell me a number in base 10.

77 in base 10 is 1001101 base 2.

77

Figure 1-2: Converting 77_{10} into base 2

Because of the way Scratch works, you'll see a lot of figures in this book that combine different points from a program's execution into one image, like this one. In this case, you can see Scratch Cat's speech bubbles from both the ask and wait and say blocks, as well as the box for entering the base 10 number. The execution flow will be clear when you're doing these experiments yourself, but when you're looking at the figures in the book you might need to do a little interpretation of what happens when.

Hacking the Code

The program treats the decimal-to-binary conversion as a sequence of halvings. You could also think of it in reverse, as a sequence of doublings, with a +1 for each 1 in the binary representation and a +0 for each 0. For example, we can represent the conversion of 77 mathematically as:

$$77_{10} = (((((1 \cdot 2 + 0) \cdot 2 + 0) \cdot 2 + 1) \cdot 2 + 1) \cdot 2 + 0) \cdot 2 + 1$$
$$= 1001101_2$$

You can see the digits of the binary representation in red. Stacking up the multiplications in this way puts every binary digit with its appropriate power of 2.

Another important thing to know about this program is that while the answer Scratch reports looks like a number, it's actually a string. As I mentioned earlier, a string is just a list of characters. Usually those characters are letters of the alphabet strung together to form messages like Hello or Tell me a number, but in this case, the characters happen to be 0s and 1s. So even though the result looks like binary digits making up a number, Scratch has no idea that 1001101 is a binary number with a decimal value of 77.

We have to use strings because Scratch doesn't have a built-in way to work directly with binary numbers. If we wanted Scratch to do binary arithmetic on base 2 numbers, we would have to write a custom program to teach it how. This is the first of many cases in this book where we'll have to treat numbers as strings to "trick" Scratch into doing what we want.

Programming Challenges

1.1 Write a program that prompts for a base *b*, then prompts for a base 10 number *n*, and then returns the number *n* written in the base *b*. You might limit the base *b* to be between 2 and 10, or go on to use the digits E and T to allow base 11 or 12.

1.2 A popular computer-related base is base 16, *hexadecimal*, which usually uses the extra symbols A, B, C, D, E, and F to stand for 10, 11, 12, 13, 14, and 15. Extend your base converter to give hexadecimal representations. See if you can spot the trick for converting back and forth between binary and hexadecimal.

Project 2: What's 1001101 in Decimal?

Now let's try converting backward from a binary representation to a decimal one. Figure 1-3 shows a Scratch program that does this.

We first ask the user for a string representing a binary value with an ask and wait block. Then we use a repeat loop and the index variable to look at the string one character at a time, from left to right, with letter index of answer accessing the current character. The variable n starts at 0. For each digit in the binary representation, n is doubled and then has the value of the current digit (either 0 or 1) added to it. When there are no more binary digits left, n holds the decimal representation of the number.

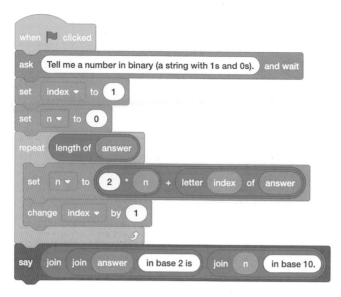

Figure 1-3: A program to convert binary (base 2) numbers into decimal (base 10)

The Results

We know that 77 in binary is 1001101. Try running the program and entering 1001101 to see if it gives 77 back. Figure 1-4 shows the results.

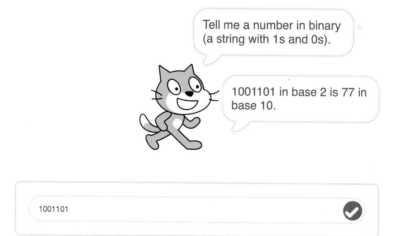

Figure 1-4: Converting 1001101$_2$ into base 10

We've worked a lot with 77, converting it to binary in Figure 1-2 and then back to decimal again in Figure 1-4. But what is the number 77 *really*? Whether we write it in binary or decimal, 77 represents the same quantity. How we choose to write a number might reveal interesting facts about it (for instance, if a number written in decimal ends in a 0, the number must be divisible by 10, and if a number written in binary ends in a 0, the number has to be divisible by 2), but it doesn't change the value of the number at all.

Hacking the Code

One problem with our binary-to-decimal program is that it has no check to make sure it's working with a string of binary digits. If you input something that isn't a number in binary notation, Scratch Cat is happy to tell you nonsense, as the examples in Figure 1-5 show.

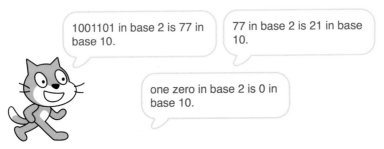

Figure 1-5: Three outputs from the binary-to-decimal converter. There's nothing to stop you from entering something other than a binary number!

We could fix this by including a custom Screen string block to check the input. This block, shown in Figure 1-6, makes sure the input is in the right form: a string of characters that includes only 0s and 1s.

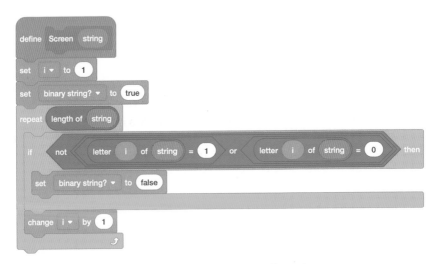

Figure 1-6: Making sure only base 2 numbers are allowed

The block sets the logical (*Boolean*, or true/false) variable `binary string?` to true as long as the user didn't input any other characters (like spaces, letters, or digits greater than 1). Otherwise, it sets `binary string?` to `false`. We can now use this block with an `if...else` statement so we don't get any silly, incorrect answers, as shown in Figure 1-7. The operator blocks that Scratch uses for Boolean tests are all green hexagons that you can plug into the test condition in control blocks.

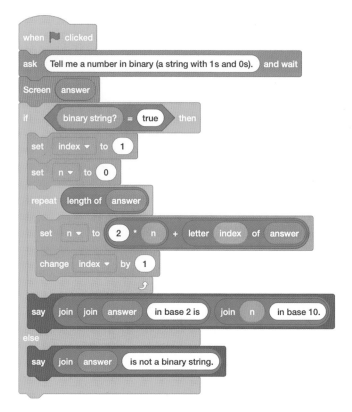

Figure 1-7: The binary-to-decimal converter done more carefully

Here, we've moved the original binary-to-decimal code inside the `if` branch of an `if...else` block so it runs only if the `binary string?` variable is `true`. Otherwise, Scratch Cat will inform the user that the input wasn't a binary number.

You may be disappointed that the program is a little longer now than it was originally. Scratch makes it easy to write really compact programs, and it even encourages this by telling you how many blocks there are in the programming window. But sometimes, it's better to be careful even if it makes your program a bit longer. If it's possible to misunderstand something or make a mistake in the input, at some point someone will do that, so it's better to be safe than sorry! Some programming languages have special commands to intercept errors and reroute them somewhere harmless (the syntax usually involves the keywords `try` and `catch`), but Scratch leaves it up to you to anticipate problems and guard against them, as we've done with the `Screen string` block.

Programming Challenge

1.3   Sometimes news stories talk about *exponential growth* as a general term to suggest rapid increase. Exponential growth means something specific in mathematics, where progression from one value in a se-. quence of numbers to the next value is done by multiplication using a fixed factor. For example, every number might be two times larger than the one before it. An alternative is *linear growth*, where the change happens by *adding* a fixed increment, such as when each number is two more than the previous one.

Write some Scratch code that prompts the user for a multiplier or an increment, and answers with a sequence of numbers that grows exponentially or linearly. Compare the growth: What happens if the user gives a number less than 1 for exponential growth? What happens if the user gives a number less than 0 for linear growth? Maybe this is a situation that calls for input screening.

How Computers Represent Numbers

Computers can represent numbers internally in different ways, but they all involve some kind of compromise. Earlier I mentioned that humans think of number systems like integers and real numbers as being infinite. Computers aren't built to handle infinite collections, though. They have to work within the confines of the architecture of their hardware or the logical structure of the programming language they're running.

On the hardware side, central processing units (CPUs) typically have *registers*, which are areas of the CPU that can hold and operate on a certain number of binary digits, or *bits*, at once. Programming languages are designed to allocate a fixed number of bits to represent each number, so language designers need to make decisions about what exactly those bits mean (for example, whether some represent a base and others an exponent). They also need to make decisions about things like how to represent a number as negative or positive and what to do if a number takes up more than the available space. Should the computation halt with a warning or an error, or should the representation wrap back around without complaint, possibly leading to unexpected and incorrect results?

Ultimately, we can't fit infinitely many numbers into a computer's finite space of possibilities, so "most" numbers have to be left out. This means the developers of a computer language need to decide which numbers and what kinds of numbers are interesting and important enough to include. Some people need to represent tiny numbers, the size of subatomic particles, while others need to represent massive numbers, the size of the universe, and still others need everything in between. Different languages may be designed to fill some of these needs but not others.

Beyond questions of how big or small the numbers are, language designers might also want to consider how the numbers will be used. For instance, sometimes numbers are used to count, answering questions about "How many?" In this case, the answer is often a whole number. (This comes up often enough that lots of programming languages give integers their own representation system, separate from other kinds of numbers.) Other times, numbers are used to measure, answering questions about "How much?" The answers to those questions are less likely to be whole numbers. Language designers need a way to represent those "in between" numbers, and they have to decide exactly how far "in between" to go.

The Point of Floating Point

Floating-point notation allows for "in between" numbers by including powers of the base smaller than 1. In base 10, there's a *decimal point*, with digits to the right of the decimal point representing a number between 0 and 1 with a combination of powers of 1/10, 1/100, and so on. For instance, the approximation of π, 3.14, indicates a number that's a little more than 3:

$$3.14 = 3 + \left(1 \cdot \frac{1}{10}\right) + \left(4 \cdot \frac{1}{100}\right)$$

If you need a closer approximation, you can include a few more digits:

$$3.1416 = 3 + \left(1 \cdot \frac{1}{10}\right) + \left(4 \cdot \frac{1}{100}\right) + \left(1 \cdot \frac{1}{1,000}\right) + \left(6 \cdot \frac{1}{10,000}\right)$$

The same principle applies to floating-point notation for binary numbers, where digits to the right of the *binary point* (the binary equivalent of a decimal point) represent powers of 1/2. You're probably familiar with using binary fractions to represent numbers—even if you don't realize it—if you've ever measured lengths with a ruler or tape measure (see Figure 1-8).

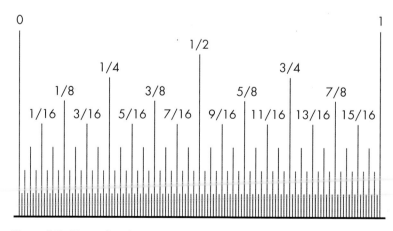

Figure 1-8: Binary fractions on a tape measure

Inches are subdivided into halves (1/2), quarters (1/4), eighths (1/8), sixteenths (1/16), and so on. These are binary fractions in that each denominator is a power of 2. You could measure 1 13/16 inches, for example, by going over 1, then 1/2, then 1/4, then 1/16, and write 1 13/16 with a binary representation of 1.1101.

Binary fractions give us a way to write non-whole numbers, but how many bits should be used to represent a number, and how should they be interpreted? Anyone who invents a computer language can make their own rules, but it's better to have a standard that everyone agrees to use so there won't be any confusion when switching from one language to another. One such standard is the IEEE Standard for Floating-Point Arithmetic, or IEEE 754. The makers of Scratch chose to use this standard to represent all numbers, even whole numbers, whereas some languages use IEEE 754 for floating-point numbers and a different standard for integers.

Double the Precision, Double the Fun

IEEE 754 uses *double precision*, meaning a floating-point number in binary will occupy 64 bits (unlike *single precision*, which allows for 32 bits per number). Figure 1-9 shows how the 64 bits are allocated.

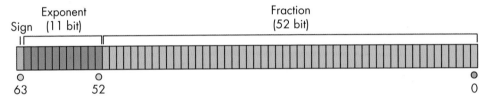

Figure 1-9: How bits are allocated in the IEEE 754 standard

The first bit, shown in cyan in the figure, is for the sign: 0 or 1 for plus or minus. The last 64 – 1 – 11 = 52 bits, shown in orange, represent a number, conventionally a value between 1 and 2, that is called the *mantissa*. Since a binary number between 1 and 2 always looks like a 1, then a binary point, then some other digits, we can save one binary digit by not writing the initial 1 explicitly. So instead of 52 bits of precision, we really have 53 bits. The 11 bits after the sign bit, colored in purple in the figure, are for the exponent, specifying a power of 2 used to multiply the mantissa. Sometimes the exponent is called the *characteristic*. Having 11 bits in the characteristic gives a range of 2^{11} possible exponents, which are interpreted as going from $2^{-1,023}$ to $2^{1,024}$, but the very top and bottom numbers are reserved for special use.

NOTE *For a hands-on look at how IEEE 754 works, there are interactive online tools that let you change floating-point numbers bit by bit (literally) to see what happens. Some examples are the double-precision tools at* https://float.exposed *and* http://evanw.github.io/float-toy/.

Keep in mind that 53 digits of precision in binary doesn't translate into 53 digits of precision in decimal. For example, $2^{10} = 1,024$, which is about the same as $10^3 = 1,000$. This indicates that 10 binary digits convey about as much information as 3 decimal digits, so 53 binary digits can hold as much information as about 16 or 17 decimal digits. That's still a lot—way more than you're likely to see on a calculator screen—but it's far from infinite.

In this book, we're mainly interested in integers, so 16 decimal digits of precision means that a 16-digit number, somewhere in the low quadrillions, is the biggest number Scratch can be counted on to represent exactly as a counting number. When we test numbers for properties such as divisibility in future chapters, we'll need to be sure all the digits of the numbers are reliably represented to get correct results. We'll explore this limitation in our next project.

Project 3: $2^{53} + 1 = ?$

Some languages give the largest integer that can be represented exactly in floating-point notation a special name, *flintmax*, which is an abbreviation for *floating-point integer maximum*. The value of flintmax in Scratch is:

$$2^{53} = 9,007,199,254,740,992$$

Figure 1-10 shows a little program illustrating how arithmetic goes awry when you try to work with numbers bigger than flintmax. Keep an eye on the variables as you run the program to see where the problem arises.

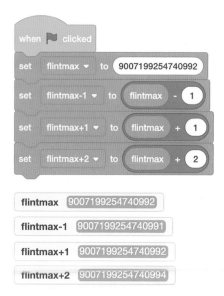

Figure 1-10: Integer arithmetic is unreliable above flintmax.

Subtracting 1 from flintmax works fine, but adding 1 to flintmax doesn't give the expected result. The value of the variable `flintmax+1` is flintmax itself. You have to add 2 to change flintmax and get a correct answer.

Hacking the Code

It's always interesting to test the limits and see where a computer language or other system breaks down. People who are interested in video games, for example, spend lots of time looking for glitches and locations that break the game's underlying model or make the game's objects behave weirdly. It's part of the fun to see how things can go wrong and to conduct experiments to try to work out how the computer is handling itself.

In this case, our program showed that when calculations in Scratch exceed flintmax, the results are suspect and may not correspond to exact integer arithmetic. We'll need to keep that in mind as we design programs to explore integer arithmetic in Scratch. As long as the numbers, including intermediate results, remain under flintmax, though, the results will be exact. For instance, you can write a Scratch program that counts up starting from 1, and you'll get all the way to flintmax before there's a missing integer value.

Our program also showed that IEEE 754 can represent *some* integers above flintmax, such as flintmax + 2, correctly. In fact, it can represent even numbers (multiples of 2) above flintmax exactly for a while, but eventually it loses another digit of binary accuracy, after which point it represents only multiples of 4 exactly. You can try extending the program in Figure 1-10 to illustrate this. What's the largest integer n for which Scratch can correctly distinguish between n and $n + 2$? How does that value compare with flintmax? Likewise, what's the largest integer n where there's a difference between n and $n + 4$?

Another way that arithmetic can get broken in Scratch is when the result of a computation doesn't match any numerical value. For example, Scratch reports Infinity when you try to divide by 0, as in Figure 1-11.

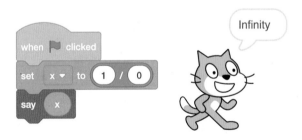

Figure 1-11: Sometimes the answer is Infinity.

But what happens when you try to subtract Infinity from Infinity? The answer reported in Figure 1-12 is NaN, which means *not a number*.

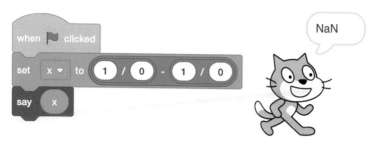

Figure 1-12: Sometimes the answer is not a number.

We'll encounter these special values, Infinity and NaN, in the output of some of our programs.

Programming Challenges

1.4   What's the largest number that Scratch can represent, integer or not? What happens when that number is exceeded?

1.5   Try using Scratch to create a floating-point simulator like the ones mentioned in the note on page 12. You should be able to look at a 64-bit string of 0s and 1s and see the floating-point number associated with it, then change the bits to see how the number changes.

Project 4: A Million-Digit Number?

In this project, we'll trick Scratch into doing exact integer arithmetic with many more digits of precision than flintmax provides. To get around the limits of the IEEE 754 standard for number representation, we'll have to program our own alternative representation system for large numbers. We have a few different options here. For example, we could store decimal numbers one digit at a time in a list, in which case the only limit would be Scratch's maximum list length of 200,000. If we stored five digits at a time as list entries, we could get to one million digits!

Another option could be to store the numbers as strings. Strings can be very long, even millions of characters. Scratch doesn't provide any built-in operations for performing arithmetic on strings, though, so if we wanted to work with numbers represented as strings we'd have to program the arithmetic operations ourselves.

Figure 1-13 shows an example of a program that reliably performs calculations on numbers well beyond flintmax. The program prompts for an exponent n and then displays all the digits of 2^n, both as a list of digits and as a string built by joining the digits together.

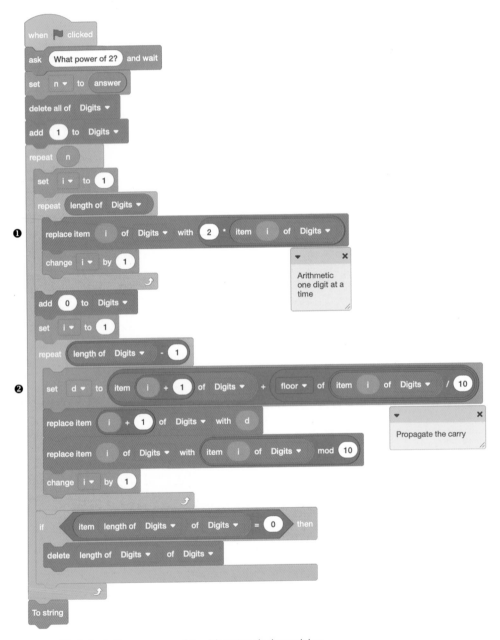

Figure 1-13: Calculating powers of 2 with extended precision

The program builds up 2^n as a list of digits from right to left. The list (called Digits) starts with just the number 1, which is 2^0. Then we repeat the process of doubling n times, calculating the next highest power of 2 by stepping through each digit in the list (using the i variable) and doubling it ❶. A problem comes up for digits with values between 5 and 9, though, which double into two-digit numbers.

To solve this problem, think about how addition works. In particular, consider how you're taught to add multidigit numbers from right to left while keeping track of a *carry*. If you wanted to calculate 24 + 18, for example, you would start with the ones digit, so you would calculate 4 + 8 = 12, write down 2, and carry the 1. Then you would look at the tens digit; you would calculate 2 + 1 = 3, add the carry to get 4, and then report the answer as 42. The 1 that was carried in the first step was actually 10, so it counts as 1 · 10 when we keep track of the groups of 10 counted in the leftmost place.

The second nested repeat loop ❷ in Figure 1-13 implements this carrying logic to limit every number in the list to a single digit. Calculating floor of item i of Digits / 10 gives us 1 if the current number has two digits. We add that 1 to the next item in the list (item i + 1) to perform the carry, then take item i of Digits mod 10 to limit the current number to just its ones digit. Before all this, we add a 0 to the end of the list in case the last item needs a carry operation. The if...then statement near the end of the program removes that 0 if it wasn't needed.

Hacking the Code

It would be nice to see the answer reported so it looks like a number, not a digit-by-digit list. We can do that with the custom To string block shown in Figure 1-14.

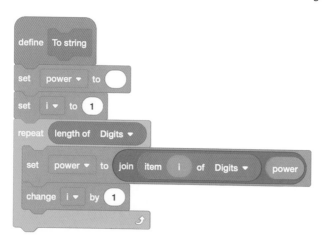

Figure 1-14: Merging the list of digits into a string

This block joins the items of the list into a string, building it up from right to left, so the answer is exhibited in a more readable way.

The Results

Try testing the program on a bigger number than Scratch would normally be able to represent. For example, Figure 1-15 shows a run of the program calculating 2^{106}, which is flintmax squared.

Figure 1-15: Accurately calculating flintmax squared

All 32 digits are reported correctly (after Scratch finishes, you can scroll down through the list to see them all). Notice that Digits lists the digits starting from the ones place.

Programming Challenges

1.6 Modify the power of 2 code in Figure 1-13 to calculate 3^{53}.

1.7 Modify the power of 2 code in Figure 1-13 so it works on "digits" that are between 0 and 99,999. That makes each list entry give five digits of the calculated power, allowing Scratch to hold up to one million digits.

1.8 Program an extended precision addition, where Scratch Cat prompts for two large numbers entered as strings, resolves the numbers as lists of digits, and then adds the numbers using the same technique as the program in Figure 1-13. Try to extend the code to handle multiplication as well.

Conclusion

If we understand how Scratch keeps track of numbers, we can be sure to avoid generating errors by asking for more than Scratch can give us. This will be especially important for integer arithmetic, where we need all the digits of a number to correctly manage questions about divisibility and counting.

Scratch's internal representation of numbers matches that of many modern programming languages, so the information in this chapter is widely applicable. Once we know the limits, we can figure out how to work around them to get more information out of a program than the language could normally provide. That's the best hack of all!

2

Exploring Divisibility and Primes

You can add, subtract, or multiply any two integers and get an integer back. But when you divide one integer by another, the answer doesn't have to be an integer. The special case when the result of the division *is* an integer is worth noticing. Also notable are those rare cases where a number can't be cleanly divided by any numbers besides 1 and itself. We call those *prime numbers*.

In this chapter, we'll investigate these two interesting phenomena. These concepts are fundamental to *number theory*, the study of the properties and mathematics of integers. Number theory is used for everything from random number generation in computer games and simulations to designing error-correcting codes for data transmission and storage. These real-world applications all start with divisibility and primes.

The Divisibility Factor

We say that the integer d is a *divisor* of the integer n if the division n / d results in an integer. We can say it with multiplication as well: the number n is *divisible* by the number d if we can find an integer k so that $n = d \cdot k$. Another way to say the same thing is that d is a *factor* of n.

Here are some facts, observations, and vocabulary about divisibility:

* Every number is divisible by 1 because we can write $n = n \cdot 1$.
* Every number n is a divisor (or factor) of itself. If we don't want to include n in the list of divisors, we can specify the others as *proper divisors*.
* Integers are *even* or *odd* depending on whether they're divisible by 2.
* Every integer divisible by 5 is guaranteed to have a last digit of 0 or 5.
* Every integer divisible by 10 ends in a 0.
* The set of positive divisors of 6 is {1, 2, 3, 6}. The number 6 is considered *perfect* because the sum of its proper divisors, 1 + 2 + 3, is 6 itself.

Programming Challenge

2.1 Fizz-Buzz is a game that can be played by any number of players seated in a circle. Players take turns counting up from 1, but if the number they're supposed to say is divisible by 5, the player says "Fizz" instead of the number. If the number is divisible by 7, the player says "Buzz." If the number is divisible by both 5 and 7, the player says "Fizz Buzz." If a player says the wrong thing, they're out, and the last player left wins. Write a program so Scratch Cat can play Fizz-Buzz with you.

Modular Arithmetic

Even though dividing one integer by another doesn't necessarily result in another integer, *modular arithmetic* gives us a way to express any division operation using integers. The answer to a modular division problem is reported as two separate integers: the *quotient* itself, with any decimal component removed, and an extra part called the *remainder*. Symbolically, we say the integer b divided by the positive integer a gives a quotient q and a remainder r, where $0 \leq r < a$. The relationship is given by the equation $b = (q \cdot a) + r$.

Division is the process of determining a quotient and remainder given b and a. The *division algorithm* identifies the quotient and remainder. Scratch has a built-in operation to capture the remainder r, called mod. To find the quotient q, we do the division using the / operator and indicate that we want to keep only the integer part of the result by using the floor operation. Figure 2-1 gives an example.

Figure 2-1: Calculating the quotient and remainder of 45/7

Here, floor of 45 / 7 gives us a quotient of 6, and 45 mod 7 gives us a remainder of 3. To check this is right, we can plug the results into our formula:

$$b = (q \cdot a) + r$$
$$= (6 \cdot 7) + 3$$
$$= 42 + 3$$
$$= 45$$

We say two numbers x and y are *congruent modulo n* if x mod $n = y$ mod n. In this case, when x and y are divided by n, they have the same remainder r. For example, 7 and 19 are congruent mod 6 because 7 and 19 divided by 6 both yield a remainder of 1. Congruence isn't as strong as equality, in that equal numbers must be congruent, but congruent numbers need not be equal. Instead of an equal sign (=), we use the triple bar symbol ($\equiv$) for congruence, so we write $7 \equiv 19$ mod 6.

Here are some facts connecting modular arithmetic to divisibility:

* We can test for divisibility of b by a with Scratch by seeing if b mod a is 0.

* Odd numbers are all congruent to 1 mod 2, and even numbers are congruent to 0 mod 2.

* Numbers that end in 0 are congruent to 0 mod 10. They're also divisible by 10.

* Numbers that end in 0 or 5 are congruent to 0 mod 5. They're also divisible by 5.

* When we represent $b = (q \cdot a) + r$ by the division algorithm, the set of all possible remainders is $\{0, 1, 2, \ldots, a - 1\}$, a set of a elements. Sometimes it's more useful to use another set of a elements where every integer is congruent to one element of the set. Since Scratch numbers elements in lists starting from 1, the set $\{1, 2, 3, \ldots, a\}$ is often a good choice.

We'll explore a simple hack that uses modular arithmetic to help check the results of a calculation in the next project.

Project 5: A Trick for Checking Your Math

Casting out nines is a trick for verifying the answer to a large addition or multiplication problem. To see how it works, first notice that every power of 10 leaves a remainder of 1 when it's divided by 9. For example:

$$10 = 9 + 1$$
$$100 = 99 + 1 = (11 \cdot 9) + 1$$
$$1{,}000 = 999 + 1 = (111 \cdot 9) + 1$$

This points to a broader rule that when you divide a number n by 9, you get the same remainder as when you divide the sum of the digits of n by 9. Take the case of 347 divided by 9. To determine the remainder, we first sum the digits: 3 + 4 + 7 = 14. At this point, we could notice that 14 = (1 · 9) + 5, giving us a remainder of 5. Or we could do the casting out nines trick a second time to get the result in an easier way: 1 + 4 = 5. (In fact, 347 divided by 9 is 38 remainder 5.)

Casting out nines is a good way to check your work after a big addition or multiplication operation because it's much easier to do arithmetic mod 9 (by summing a number's digits) than to keep track of multidigit sums and products. Suppose, for example, you calculate 347 + 264 and get the answer 601. We've already seen that 347 mod 9 is 5. For 264, 2 + 6 + 4 = 12 and 1 + 2 = 3, so 264 mod 9 is 3. That means (347 + 264) mod 9 should be 5 + 3 = 8. But 601 mod 9 is 6 + 0 + 1 = 7, so something is wrong. It looks like somebody forgot to carry the 1 in the original addition! When we fix the sum to be 611, casting out nines works as expected.

Even though adding up the digits of a number is pretty easy mental math, let's have Scratch Cat do the work for us. The program in Figure 2-2 uses the casting out nines technique to find any number mod 9.

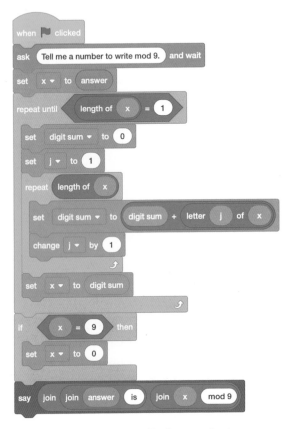

Figure 2-2: A program for finding x mod 9 by calculating digit sums

The trick is to have Scratch see the number x as a string of digits. The length of operator reports how many digits the number has, and the letter of operator lets us pick off one digit at a time so we can add them up. The code is nested inside a repeat until loop that makes it continue until the length of x is 1, meaning the number has only one digit. If that single digit is in the range 0 through 8, we have our answer. The single digit could also be a 9, though, which is congruent to 0 mod 9. In that case, the last if statement picks 0 as the answer to report instead of 9.

The Results

Figure 2-3 shows a sample run of the program, using 601 as the input.

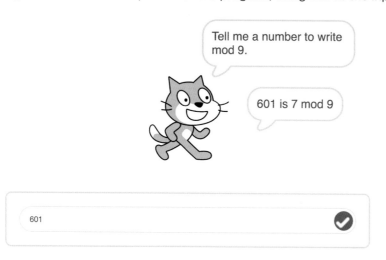

Figure 2-3: Finding 601 mod 9

The last line of the program uses join operations to make the output pretty, reminding us of the input number and the result of the casting out nines process.

Hacking the Code

We have the same problem here that we had in Chapter 1: Scratch is happy to run the code on input that isn't a number. The way the program is written, it even gets in trouble with what ought to be perfectly allowable inputs, like negative integers. For example, the number –3 interpreted as a string has a length of 2, and according to Scratch, the first character, the minus sign, has a numerical value of 0. So Scratch reports that the sum of the digits of –3 is 0 + 3 = 3. The trouble is that –3 mod 9 is equal to 6, not 3.

Because we'll run into problems with negative integers and non-integer inputs, before we put the code out for general use, we should make it safe by screening possible inputs to allow only the ones we want: positive integers. We can create a custom block to screen the input, as shown in Figure 2-4.

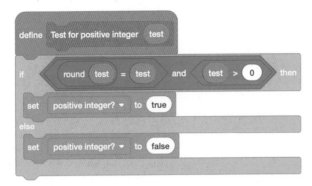

Figure 2-4: Making sure the input is a positive integer

The Boolean statement round test = test is a hack that lets us kill a few birds with one stone. It screens out non-numeric input (such as the word *banana*), since trying to round a non-number in Scratch produces 0 as a result. It also screens out numbers with nonzero decimal components, which will no longer be equal to themselves after rounding. Combined with text > 0, our if statement is true if the input test is a positive integer and false otherwise, so we can set the value of the variable positive integer? to true if the two conditions are satisfied.

NOTE   *Some programming languages have special Boolean variables that can take on only the values true or false, but Scratch doesn't. Here, we simply use the words true and false instead. Some programmers prefer to use the numerical values 1 and 0 to keep track of truth values.*

Once we have a screening block, we can modify the code in Figure 2-2 to execute for only appropriate values, as shown in Figure 2-5. Paste the original program from the repeat until block onward into the empty slot after the if.

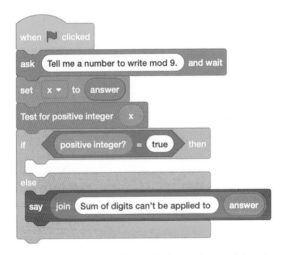

Figure 2-5: Don't let Scratch Cat make a mistake!

Of course, you don't actually have to go through the casting out nines process to perform this calculation. You can just use Scratch's mod block! Still, writing the program is good practice for figuring out how to solve a problem and how to analyze a number one digit at a time. The program also generalizes to other cases, such as the one in Challenge 2.2.

Programming Challenges

2.2   Casting out nines gives a test for divisibility by 9, since if the sum of the digits is 0 or 9, the number is divisible by 9. A test for divisibility by 11 works similarly, except instead of adding all the digits, you alternately subtract and add them. For example, 1,342 is divisible by 11 because 1 − 3 + 4 − 2 = 0. Program Scratch to calculate the −/+ digit sum for a given number to see if it's divisible by 11.

2.3   Scratch has an operator that lets you pick a random number in a specified range. Write a program to pick 10 random numbers between 1 and 100. Predict how many are likely to be divisible by 9, then use Scratch to check if your prediction was right.

2.4   Sometimes when you have to enter a number into a computer form (like a credit card number or a book's ISBN code), the number includes a *check digit* to make sure you haven't made a mistake. One way to implement this is to add an extra digit at the end that's derived from the original number. For example, the extra digit could be the original number mod 9, found by casting out nines as in the program in Figure 2-2. Extend this program to give the original number with its check digit added.

2.5   When copying numbers we sometimes make *transposition* errors, where two digits are switched. For example, we might miswrite 1,467 as 1,647. Could you use the casting out nines trick to help catch this kind of mistake?

Prime Numbers

Some integers have many divisors, and some have only a few. The integer 1 is a special case, in that it's divisible only by itself. For any other number, the smallest number of divisors is two: 1 and the number itself. As mentioned at the beginning of this chapter, numbers with only two divisors are called prime numbers. Numbers with more than two divisors are called *composite numbers*.

The first few prime numbers are 2, 3, 5, 7, 11, 13, and 17. To find more, we'll turn to Scratch.

One way to determine if a number is prime is to try out possible factors one by one, a process called *trial division*. If there aren't any other divisors between 1 and the number, then the number is prime. For the number 5, for example, we would try dividing 5 by 2, then 3, then 4. None of those numbers divide evenly into 5, so 5 is prime.

Doing trial division manually quickly gets tedious, so we'll write a program to make Scratch do it for us. Figure 2-6 shows a simple version of the code that doesn't worry about improper inputs that could cause incorrect answers (for example, strings or numbers that aren't positive integers).

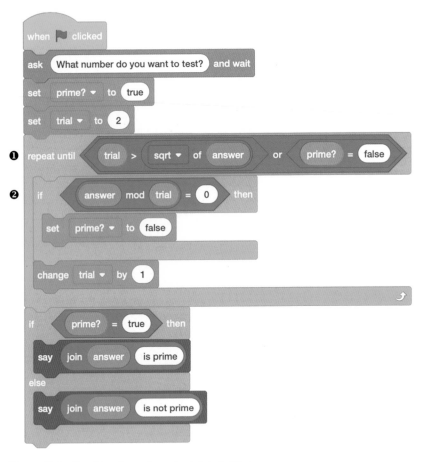

Figure 2-6: Checking for primes by trial division

The code prompts for a number to test and decides if the number is prime by working with the Boolean prime? variable. We perform the trial division in a repeat until loop ❶ by calculating answer mod trial ❷, where the variable trial is the trial divisor. If the result is 0, we know that we have a divisor and that answer isn't prime, so we exit the loop. Otherwise, we add 1 to trial and try again. At the end, we report an answer based on whether prime? is true or false.

The Results

Figure 2-7 shows some sample runs of the trial division program.

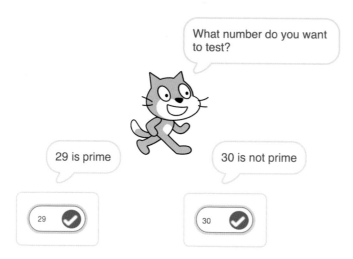

Figure 2-7: Sample runs of the trial division program

The program correctly identifies 29 as prime and 30 as not prime.

Hacking the Code

We should screen the input so Scratch is considering only positive integers. A custom block like the one we made for the casting out nines program (see Figure 2-4) would work, put into an if statement (as in Figure 2-5). There are a few more conditions to put into the screening code, though. First, the integer 1 is neither prime nor composite, but 1 would survive the repeat until loop in our trial division program and be labeled as prime. The custom block in Figure 2-8 includes an initial if test to disallow an input of 1.

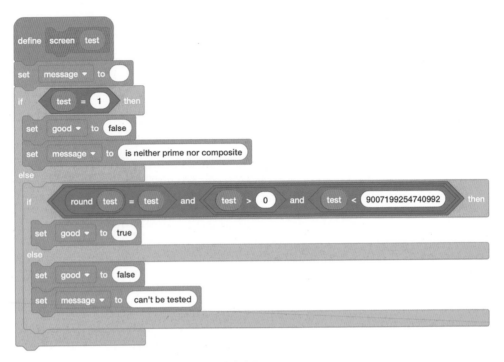

Figure 2-8: Limiting the input for the trial division program

A more subtle problem is that, as we saw in Chapter 1, integer arithmetic is exact only up to flintmax. That means the divisibility test works only for numbers up to 9,007,199,254,740,992. After that, Scratch Cat thinks every number is composite! The check code in Figure 2-8 accounts for this as well by verifying that test is less than flintmax. The block also returns a message variable giving more information for the program to report when the input can't reliably be tested.

Another consideration with this program is that trial division on large numbers potentially takes many steps—so many that even on a fast computer you might have to wait a long time to get an answer. The test in the repeat until loop ❶ in Figure 2-6 is a hack to speed up the process: we really have to consider only trial divisors up to the square root of the input number. This works because if a number n isn't prime, it must have a factorization $n = a \cdot b$ other than the trivial factorization $1 \cdot n$. Since $n = \sqrt{n} \cdot \sqrt{n}$, one of a or b must be at least as big as $\sqrt{n}$ and the other must be $\sqrt{n}$ or smaller. We have to do trial division only up to $\sqrt{n}$ to find the smaller one, if it exists.

This hack provides a huge savings! We can test numbers up to 1,000,000 with no more than $\sqrt{1,000,000} = 1,000$ trial divisions. To speed up the code even further, once we've checked on divisibility by 2, we could test only for divisibility by odd numbers. This is because if a number n is divisible by any even number, it will also be divisible by 2.

All these improvements allow for shorter runtimes, but they also make for a longer, more complicated program. Whether the trade-off is worth it will depend on who will be using your work, and for what. Improvements that make the program easier to use are usually worth it. Improvements that speed up runtime have to be dramatic to be noticeable, but they may be worthwhile if users will be looking for quick results.

Project 7: The Sieve of Eratosthenes

Trial division isn't the only way to find prime numbers. In this project, we'll explore a different technique: looking at a list of all numbers up to some limit and throwing away the numbers that are composite. This approach sifts, or *sieves*, out the primes and is called the *sieve of Eratosthenes* after the Greek mathematician who first used it. Scratch Cat uses sieving in Figure 2-9, where the numbers 1 through 120 have been arranged in a grid.

✖	2	3	4	5	6
7	8	9	10	11	12
13	14	15	16	17	18
19	20	21	22	23	24
25	26	27	28	29	30
31	32	33	34	35	36
37	38	39	40	41	42
43	44	45	46	47	48
	50	51	52	53	54
	56	57	58	59	60
	62	63	64	65	66
	68	69	70	71	72
	74	75	76	77	78
	80	81	82	83	84
85	86	87	88	89	90
91	92	93	94	95	96
97	98	99	100	101	102
103	104	105	106	107	108
109	110	111	112	113	114
115	116	117	118	119	120

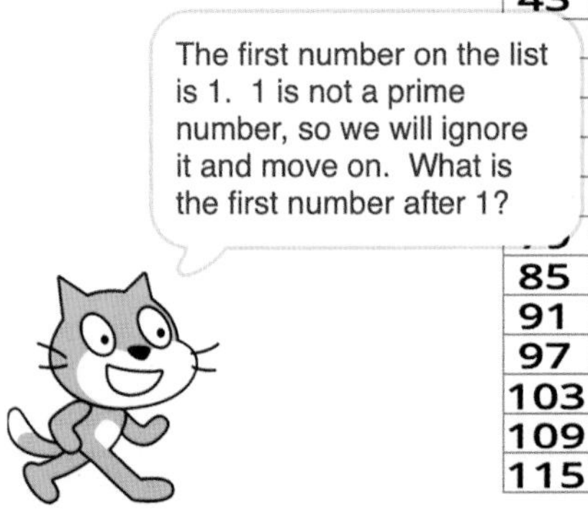

The first number on the list is 1. 1 is not a prime number, so we will ignore it and move on. What is the first number after 1?

Figure 2-9: Sieving out the primes by throwing away non-primes

First, we cross out 1, which is neither prime nor composite, in red. Then, we cross out all multiples of 2 in green, as shown on the left side of Figure 2-10, and see what's left. We continue by identifying the next few primes after 2 (3, 5, and 7) and crossing out any multiples of them, as shown on the right side of Figure 2-10.

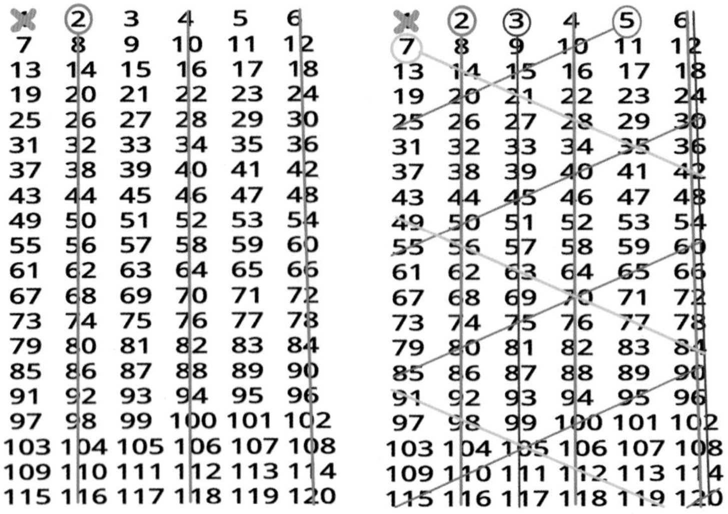

Left grid:

1	2	3	4	5	6
7	8	9	10	11	12
13	14	15	16	17	18
19	20	21	22	23	24
25	26	27	28	29	30
31	32	33	34	35	36
37	38	39	40	41	42
43	44	45	46	47	48
49	50	51	52	53	54
55	56	57	58	59	60
61	62	63	64	65	66
67	68	69	70	71	72
73	74	75	76	77	78
79	80	81	82	83	84
85	86	87	88	89	90
91	92	93	94	95	96
97	98	99	100	101	102
103	104	105	106	107	108
109	110	111	112	113	114
115	116	117	118	119	120

Right grid:

1	2	3	4	5	6
7	8	9	10	11	12
13	14	15	16	17	18
19	20	21	22	23	24
25	26	27	28	29	30
31	32	33	34	35	36
37	38	39	40	41	42
43	44	45	46	47	48
49	50	51	52	53	54
55	56	57	58	59	60
61	62	63	64	65	66
67	68	69	70	71	72
73	74	75	76	77	78
79	80	81	82	83	84
85	86	87	88	89	90
91	92	93	94	95	96
97	98	99	100	101	102
103	104	105	106	107	108
109	110	111	112	113	114
115	116	117	118	119	120

Figure 2-10: Eliminating all the even numbers after 2 (left) and all multiples of 3, 5, and 7 (right)

Notice that multiples of 2 and 3 are crossed out with vertical lines down the columns of the grid. This works because the grid is set up to be six numbers wide, and 6 is divisible by both 2 and 3. Multiples of 5, crossed out in pink, step backward on the diagonal. This is because to get from one multiple of 5 to the next multiple we add 5, which is 6 – 1. So to find the next multiple of 5, we go down one row for the 6 and back one column for the –1. Similarly, to find multiples of 7, crossed out in yellow, we go down one row and step one column to the right (because 7 = 6 + 1), giving us lines along the other diagonal.

Here's the payoff of sieving: if a number n is composite and has a factorization $n = a \cdot b$ where $1 < a \le b < n$, then $a \le \sqrt{n}$. In our example, $n = 120$, so any composite number in the grid must have a prime factor less than $\sqrt{120}$, or approximately 10.95. Once we've sieved up to 7, the next number that hasn't already been crossed out is 11, which is greater than $\sqrt{120}$, so 7 is as far as we need to sieve. Every number that remains, meaning it hasn't been crossed off as a multiple of 2, 3, 5, or 7, must be a prime number (see Figure 2-11).

This is the second time the square root hack has been useful. First, it made the trial division program in Figure 2-6 run faster. Now it's telling us when to stop sieving, allowing us (in this example) to find all primes less than 120 just by sieving up to 7.

We could use the same technique to sieve up to a much higher bound. All we have to do

	2	3		5	
7				11	
13				17	
19				23	
				29	
31					
37				41	
43				47	
				53	
				59	
61					
67				71	
73					
79				83	
				89	
97				101	
103				107	
109				113	

Figure 2-11: All the primes up to 120, after sieving

is get rid of all the multiples of each prime as they're discovered, up to the square root of the bound. That's what we do in the Scratch program in Figure 2-12.

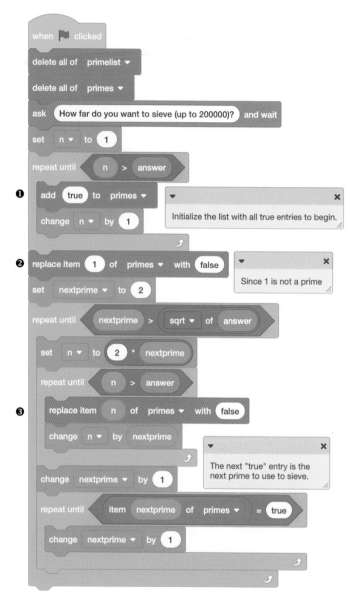

Figure 2-12: The sieve program

We start by asking how far to go, then seed the list primes with that many entries ❶. (Since we're using a list, our upper bound is limited by the maximum list size that Scratch supports, which is 200,000.) Scratch indexes lists starting with 1, so the list entry at index *n* will keep track of whether *n* is a prime. Initially we set each entry to true, but we'll change non-prime entries to false as we sieve.

First, we handle the special case of 1, which is neither prime nor composite ❷. Then, we look for the next number not crossed out by sieving so far. We leave that number as true but set all multiples of that number to false ❸. We repeat this process until the next number not crossed out is greater than the square root of the limit.

Once we have a complete list, we can access it and answer questions about the prime numbers we've found. Figure 2-13 has a little piece of code to count how many primes there are up to the sieve limit.

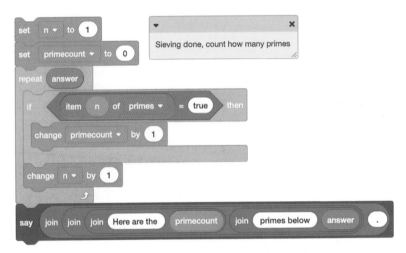

Figure 2-13: Counting primes with the sieve program

Here, we step through the list we've built and count how many true entries there are, incrementing the variable primecount each time. Figure 2-14 shows another extra piece of code that lists the primes we've found.

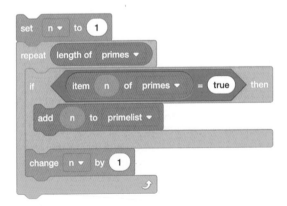

Figure 2-14: Listing primes with the sieve program

This block finds the true items in the list and stores their corresponding index numbers in a separate list.

Hacking the Code

Sometimes it's useful to have the data that Scratch generates as a separate file so you can import it into a text editor or a spreadsheet. Fortunately, Scratch gives us the option to import and export lists by right-clicking the list in the graphics window (see Figure 2-15). This way, you can take your sieved list of primes out of Scratch to play with it further.

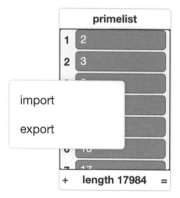

Figure 2-15: Saving the list to work on later

Text editors, word processors, and spreadsheet programs are happy to work with the text output from Scratch. Try importing your data into a spreadsheet program such as Excel, Numbers, or Open Office. If you want several entries per row, make sure you have Scratch insert commas separating the entries in your text file (using the join block), and then use the *CSV* format, short for *comma-separated values*, to import it. The default carriage returns in the file that Scratch produces will list the entries in separate rows in the spreadsheet.

Programming Challenges

2.6 Use the sieve program to find how many primes there are between 1 and 10, 100, 1,000, 10,000, and 100,000. Keep track of the ratio between the number of primes and the size of the list, and display your results in a table. How does the relative number of primes appear to be changing as the upper bound increases?

2.7 Write a block to scan the list of integers that the sieve program produces, looking for long sequences of consecutive composite numbers. What's the longest sequence you can find?

(continued)

2.8 *Twin primes* are pairs of primes that differ by exactly 2; for example, 3 and 5 or 11 and 13. Write a block to scan the sieve program's output and count how many pairs of twin primes there are up to the sieving limit.

2.9 Rewrite the sieve program in Figure 2-12 so it displays the results in a table six entries wide, like the table in Figure 2-9. Use the language of congruences to explain why the only prime numbers that appear after the first row of the table are in columns 1 and 5.

Nothing Common About Common Divisors

Given two integers a and b, the *set of common divisors* refers to all the integers that evenly divide both a and b. There will always be at least one common divisor, the number 1, since 1 is a factor of all integers. But larger common divisors might exist as well. Of particular interest is the *greatest common divisor (GCD)*, the largest number that evenly divides a and b. If this largest common divisor is d, we write GCD(a, b) = d.

As with identifying primes, there are several methods for finding the GCD of two numbers, with varying degrees of efficiency. We'll explore two such techniques in the next two projects.

Project 8: Greatest Common Divisors the Slow Way

Here's one way to find the greatest common divisor between two integers a and b. Starting from 1, try dividing a and b by every number. If it divides evenly into both of them, you've found a common divisor. Stop once you reach a or b, whichever comes first. The highest common divisor you've found is the GCD. The program in Figure 2-16 uses this approach.

We use a custom block to identify the minimum of the two input values, a and b. Then we count up from 1 to the minimum, checking if the mod of both a and b is 0. If it is, we store the current divisor in the variable gcd, which holds our answer when the program finishes running.

This technique of testing every number as a possible common divisor is known as a *brute-force* approach. It's like trying to guess someone's computer password by testing out every possible sequence of letters and numbers. For our GCD program, brute force is fast enough for smaller values of a and b, say up to 1 million, but it's noticeably slower for larger numbers. As the numbers being screened get closer to flintmax, it becomes especially annoying to wait. Luckily, there's a better way.

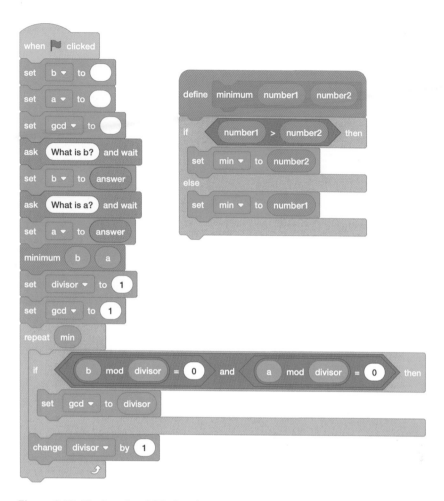

Figure 2-16: Finding the GCD the slow way

Project 9: Greatest Common Divisors the Fast Way

The Greek mathematician Euclid described a more efficient method for calculating the greatest common divisor of two numbers in his textbook *The Elements*, which was written around 300 BCE. *The Elements* covers topics in several different areas of mathematics, focusing on geometry and number theory. The book was so influential that Euclid's organization of the material was used to teach mathematics for centuries, and it continues to be used today.

Euclid's approach to calculating greatest common divisors is based on the observation that for two positive integers a and b where $a < b$, any common divisor of a and b is also a divisor of $b - a$. For example, say $a = 330$ and $b = 876$. A common divisor of 330 and 876 is 6, and 6 is also a divisor of 876 – 330 = 546.

By extension, if we divide the larger of the two numbers, b, by the smaller, a, and keep track of the division with a quotient and remainder, $b = q \cdot a + r$, then any common divisor of b and a is also a divisor of a and r. Then we can repeat the process with a and r, and so on until there's a last remainder of 0. At this point, the next-to-last remainder is the greatest common divisor of a and b. The sequence of divisions looks like this:

$$b = q_1 \cdot a + r_1$$
$$a = q_2 \cdot r_1 + r_2$$
$$r_1 = q_3 \cdot r_2 + r_3$$
$$\vdots$$
$$r_{k-2} = q_k \cdot r_{k-1} + r_k$$
$$r_{k-1} = q_{k+1} \cdot r_k + 0$$

The remainders decrease, so $a > r_1 > r_2 > \ldots > r_k$, with $r_k = \mathrm{GCD}(b, a)$ and $r_{k+1} = 0$.

Here are the steps to calculate that 6 is the greatest common divisor of $b = 876$ and $a = 330$, interpreted both with the division algorithm and with modular arithmetic. Notice how the values shift positions from right to left as we move from one line to the next:

876	=	$2 \cdot 330 + 216$		876 mod 330	=	216
330	=	$1 \cdot 216 + 114$		330 mod 216	=	114
216	=	$1 \cdot 114 + 102$		216 mod 114	=	102
114	=	$1 \cdot 102 + 12$		114 mod 102	=	12
102	=	$8 \cdot 12 + 6$		102 mod 12	=	6
12	=	$2 \cdot 6 + 0$		12 mod 6	=	0

The Scratch program in Figure 2-17 implements Euclid's algorithm.

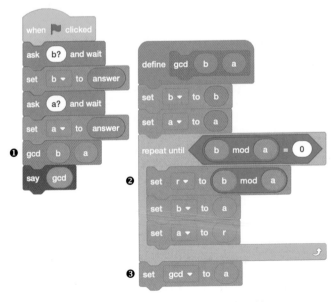

Figure 2-17: Finding the GCD with Euclid's algorithm

The program is organized so all the work of the repeated division occurs in the custom gcd block ❶. The block's definition is surprisingly short compared to our brute-force GCD program (Figure 2-16). Inside a repeat until loop, we keep taking b mod a ❷ and shuffling the values of a and r back into b and a until we finally get down to a remainder of 0. That's where the loop stops, and the last value of a can be reported as the GCD ❸.

The Results

Figure 2-18 shows a sample run of the GCD program with two very large numbers as inputs.

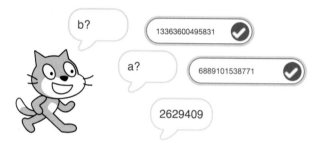

Figure 2-18: A calculation with Euclid's algorithm

Unlike our brute-force approach, the code works very quickly, even for numbers close to flintmax.

Hacking the Code

So far, the language we've used to talk about how efficient an algorithm is has been pretty general. We talk about a program running quickly or slowly, but it would be good to know just how quickly or slowly that turns out to be on your computer. It would also be useful to see how the program's performance changes as we go from working with numbers in the tens or hundreds to numbers in the thousands or millions.

Scratch has a built-in timer that measures elapsed time in seconds from the moment a program starts executing. It's accessible via the timer block in the Sensing section of the block menu. We can take any program and wrap it in a few lines of code to time how long an algorithm takes to run, as shown in Figure 2-19.

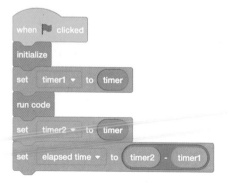

Figure 2-19: Timing how fast a program runs

Here, the initialize block would contain any setup code that you don't want to time, such as prompting the user for input, while the run code block would contain the code for the algorithm you want to time. We record the value of timer before and after executing run code, then take the difference between the two times to see how long the execution took.

Figure 2-20 shows the result of wrapping the trial division prime testing program from Figure 2-6 in the timer code, including the value of elapsed time when the program finishes. For a prime close to flintmax, it takes my computer a little over a minute to report.

Figure 2-20: Testing a big prime number

For many programs with small test values, the elapsed time will show as 0, since the algorithm takes only a fraction of a second to run. The reported time might also vary across runs because your computer is doing other things in the background, which limits the amount of resources Scratch has available to do its job. To get an accurate time, run the program lots of times in a row and keep track of the cumulative runtime, then divide by the number of times you ran the program to find the average time for each run.

Programming Challenges

2.10 Use timing loops to compare the runtimes for the two GCD calculating programs (the brute-force version in Figure 2-16 and the Euclidean version in Figure 2-17).

2.11 Program a counter to count how many steps Euclid's algorithm takes. Experiment to see what numbers make the algorithm take the highest number of steps to run.

Conclusion

Computations involving divisibility are much easier and faster to do with computer assistance. If I had to work out if a number was prime by doing trial division by hand, I would probably give up after a few dozen calculations. Even if I were punching possible divisors into a calculator, I would get bored pretty quickly and probably start making mistakes ("trial and error" is mostly error!). But Scratch Cat is eager to help out for as long as I want. Scratch is a telescope that lets us look deeper into the universe of numbers than we could ever do ourselves. All we have to do is ask.

3

Splitting Numbers with Prime Factorization

Prime numbers are like the chemical elements of the world of positive integers. They're basic building blocks that can be used to produce other positive integers.

The science of chemistry teaches us that a few substances, the elements, make up everything in the world. Atoms of elements combine to make other substances called compounds, but an element's atoms can't be split apart without losing their physical properties. Similarly, we can combine prime numbers (through multiplication) to make any composite number we might want, and prime numbers can't be divided any further, since a prime number's only factors are itself and 1.

In this chapter, we'll explore *prime factorization*, the process of identifying the prime numbers that can be multiplied together to produce a given composite number. We'll consider how a number can be written as a product of primes and examine some of the interesting things we can learn from a number's prime factors.

The Fundamental Theorem of Arithmetic

It's an important fact about primes—so important that it's called the *fundamental theorem of arithmetic*—that every composite number has its own unique set of prime factors. In this sense, multiplication and addition are quite different. If you want to get 16 as an answer by adding smaller numbers, there are lots of ways to do it: 2 + 14, 5 + 11, 3 + 13, 5 + 4 + 6 + 1, and so on. But if you want to write 16 as a product of prime numbers, the only way is 2 · 2 · 2 · 2. Likewise, the only way to get 20 by multiplying primes is 2 · 2 · 5, and the only way to get 54,252 is 2 · 2 · 3 · 3 · 11 · 137.

Each of these is an example of prime factorization: we've identified the unique set of prime numbers that we can multiply together to create a certain composite number. Once you know the prime factors of a number, you can find out a lot about the number's divisors and how the number relates to other numbers through common divisors or multiples. But how do we calculate a number's prime factors in the first place?

Project 10: Is It a Prime Factor?

In Project 6, we determined if a number was prime by dividing it by every integer starting from 2. We can use a similar trial division approach to find the prime factors of a number. All we need to do is keep track of the prime factors as they're revealed during the division process. Figure 3-1 shows how.

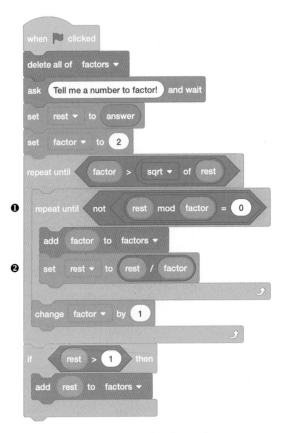

Figure 3-1: Factoring a number into primes

The program works by finding smaller prime factors first. We use two variables: rest, which starts as the number to factor, and factor, which starts as 2. If rest mod factor is 0, we've found a prime factor, so we store it in a list called factors. We then remove that factor from rest by dividing rest by factor and storing the result back into rest ❷. Next, the loop starts again using the new value of rest. When rest mod factor isn't 0, we increase factor by 1. Like when we tested for primes in Project 6, we can stop looking for factors after we reach the square root of rest ❶ because at that point, rest must be either prime or 1.

The Results

The factors list is shown on the stage, so when the program is finished, all the prime factors are displayed (maybe with scrolling, if the list gets too long). Figure 3-2 shows a sample run of the program.

Figure 3-2: Finding the prime factors of 54,252

We've successfully identified the prime factorization of 54,252 as 2 · 2 · 3 · 3 · 11 · 137. Scratch automatically numbers the elements of a list, so we can see at a glance that 54,252 has exactly six prime factors. Knowing how many prime factors a number has will come in handy later on.

Hacking the Code

Notice that a prime number can be repeated within a number's prime factorization. We can modify the code in Figure 3-1 to represent these repeated factors using exponents, since an exponent indicates repeated multiplication. For instance, instead of listing the prime factors of 54,252 as {2, 2, 3, 3, 11, 137}, we could use exponents to write the factorization as follows:

$$54{,}252 = 2^2 \cdot 3^2 \cdot 11^1 \cdot 137^1$$

Figure 3-3 shows a way to do this.

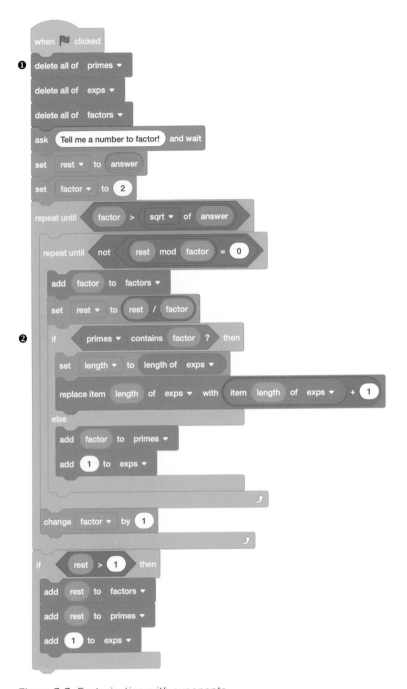

Figure 3-3: Factorization with exponents

This version of the program adds two more lists: primes keeps track of each *unique* prime number in the prime factorization, and exps keeps track of how many times each unique prime factor occurs (that is, the exponents). The program clears all the old values from the lists when it begins ❶. Then, each time a prime factor is found, we check if that factor has occurred already ❷. If it has, instead of adding it to the primes list, we increment the last exponent in the exps list by 1. If this factor hasn't occurred before, we add it to primes and add a 1 to the end of exps to represent that factor's exponent.

The lists of unique prime factors and exponents are displayed on the screen along with the original list of all the prime factors, including duplicates. Figure 3-4 shows an example with several different prime factors.

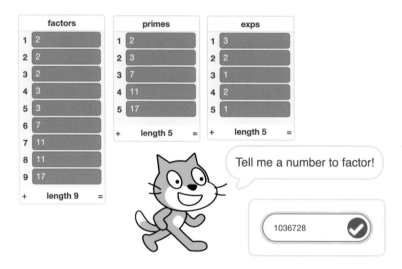

Figure 3-4: The output for a factorization with exponents

Looking at the contents of the primes and exps lists side by side, we can interpret the prime factorization of 1,036,728 as $2^3 \cdot 3^2 \cdot 7^1 \cdot 11^2 \cdot 17^1$. We'll use this modified version of the program for other projects later in this chapter, where we'll want to use the unique prime factors and their exponents to make various calculations. For those other programs, we can simply hide the lists from the Scratch stage when we don't want to see them.

Fun with Divisors

So far, we've been talking about prime *factors*, but we can also think of them as prime *divisors*—the primes that evenly divide a number. Once we format a number's prime factorization as a list of unique primes and their associated exponents, as we did in Figure 3-3, that list of unique primes is actually a list of the number's prime divisors. And once we know the *prime* divisors of a number, we can build a list of *all* the divisors of the number, not just the prime ones.

The trick is to build each divisor by multiplying the prime divisors together in different combinations, based on their exponents. For example, the prime factorization of 54 is $2^1 \cdot 3^3$. This tells us that any divisor of 54 has to be built from zero or one factors of 2 (2^0 or 2^1) and between zero and three factors of 3 (3^0, 3^1, 3^2, or 3^3). Two choices for the number of factors of 2 paired up with four choices for the number of factors of 3 gives eight ways in all to build a divisor of 54:

$$1 = 2^0 \cdot 3^0 \qquad\qquad 9 = 2^0 \cdot 3^2$$
$$2 = 2^1 \cdot 3^0 \qquad\qquad 18 = 2^1 \cdot 3^2$$
$$3 = 2^0 \cdot 3^1 \qquad\qquad 27 = 2^0 \cdot 3^3$$
$$6 = 2^1 \cdot 3^1 \qquad\qquad 54 = 2^1 \cdot 3^3$$

Zooming out from this example, we can start coming up with rules for counting how many divisors a number has. The Greek letter tau (τ) is usually used to represent the total number of divisors, so $\tau(n)$ refers to the number of divisors of the positive integer n. To start, here are some special cases:

* Prime numbers have exactly two divisors, so $\tau(p) = 2$ if p is prime.

* The only divisor of 1 is 1, so $\tau(1) = 1$.

* If p is a prime number, the divisors of p^n, some positive power of p, are $1, p, p^2, \ldots, p^n$. That means $\tau(p^n) = n + 1$. Notice that this works for the previous two special cases. For the prime number itself, $p = p^1$, so $\tau(p^1) = 1 + 1$, giving us two divisors. We can also think of $\tau(1) = 1$ as equivalent to $\tau(p^0) = 0 + 1 = 1$.

* If n is a product of two different primes, p and q, then the divisors of n are $1, p, q$, and $p \cdot q$, so $\tau(n) = 4$. A number that's a product of two prime numbers is called a *biprime*.

More broadly, how do we determine $\tau(n)$ for any composite number n? First, we can find the prime factorization of n by running n through the factorization program from Figure 3-3. That gives us two lists: a list of primes dividing n and a list of exponents. For each prime, the exponent tells us the largest possible power of the prime that divides n, so we can build a divisor of n using any number of repetitions of that prime from 0 to the exponent. Since we're counting from 0, the total number of possibilities is the exponent plus 1. So, to get $\tau(n)$, all we have to do is add 1 to each prime's exponent and multiply the results together. This is equivalent to building divisors out of every possible combination of prime factors with every possible combination of exponents.

Returning to our example of 54, we know the prime factorization is $2^1 \cdot 3^3$, so $\tau(54) = (1 + 1) \cdot (3 + 1) = 8$ divisors total. Scratch Cat agrees in Figure 3-5.

54 has 8 divisors!

Figure 3-5: Finding $\tau(54)$

But how did Scratch Cat arrive at this conclusion? Let's find out.

We can calculate $\tau(n)$, the total number of divisors of n, by adding some code to the end of the prime factorization program with exponents from Figure 3-3. Figure 3-6 shows the extra code.

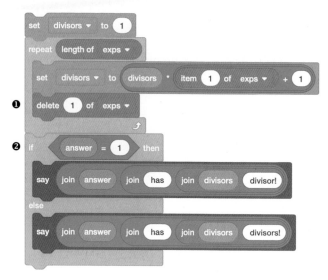

Figure 3-6: Using the exponents of n's prime factors to calculate the total number of n's divisors

After we create the list of exponents using the code from Figure 3-3, this extra code works its way through that exps list, starting from the beginning, and accumulates the total number of divisors in the divisors variable. For each exponent, we add 1 and then multiply the result by the current value of divisors. We delete each exponent from the list as we go ❶ so we can always take the first item from the list. The if...else statement ❷ just makes Scratch Cat's grammar correct, so if the user asks how many divisors the number 1 has (the only positive integer with one divisor), the answer is singular.

Project 12: Summing Up to Sigma

What if we want to find the sum of a number's divisors? The sum of the divisors of n is represented with the Greek letter sigma as $\sigma(n)$. We can use the same kind of strategy that worked for counting the number of divisors, where we keep track of one prime divisor of n and its associated exponent at a time. This is an example of *combinatorics*, a branch of mathematics sometimes called the *art of counting*, that figures out how often something can happen by analyzing simpler cases. We'll look more closely at combinatorial reasoning in Chapter 7, but for now it's a useful tool for understanding the arithmetic of divisors.

To see how to calculate $\sigma(n)$, first consider that for a given prime number p, the only divisors of the kth power of that prime are the powers of p from $p^0 = 1$

up to p^k itself. For example, the divisors of $3^3 = 27$ are 1 (3^0), 3 (3^1), 9 (3^2), and 27 (3^3). So, the sum of the divisors of 27 is:

$$\sigma(27) = 3^0 + 3^1 + 3^2 + 3^3$$
$$= 1 + 3 + 9 + 27$$
$$= 40$$

This is an example of a sum of a *geometric sequence*, a sequence of numbers where each one after the first is determined by multiplying the previous number by a constant value (in this case, 3). There's a formula for calculating the sum (or *geometric series*) of the numbers in such a sequence, $\sigma(p^k)$. In the case of adding all the powers of 3 from 3^0 to 3^3, the formula is:

$$\sigma(27) = \frac{3^4 - 1}{3 - 1} = \frac{80}{2} = 40$$

Notice that the formula involves 3^4, one exponent higher than we're looking for. More generally, if p is a prime divisor and k is its exponent, the formula for summing all the powers of p from 0 to k is:

$$\sigma(p^k) = \frac{p^{k+1} - 1}{p - 1}$$

To find the sum of all the divisors of n, all we have to do is apply this formula to each prime divisor of n and its associated exponent, then multiply all the results together. This is essentially the same trick that worked for counting the number of divisors: we're building the divisors one prime factor at a time, considering all combinations of prime factors and exponents.

Since we calculated a number's prime factors and exponents in the program in Figure 3-3, we can once again add some code to that program to sum the number's divisors. But first, because the formula hinges on calculating powers, we need a way to easily do calculations with exponents. Scratch doesn't have a built-in operator for this, so we'll have to make our own by defining a custom block, as shown in Figure 3-7.

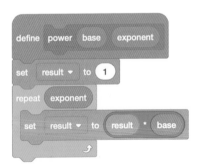

Figure 3-7: A block to calculate positive integer powers

This block takes in two values, base and exponent, and multiplies base by itself exponent number of times, storing the answer in the result variable. With the help of this block, we can now add the code shown in Figure 3-8 to the program we created earlier, in Figure 3-3.

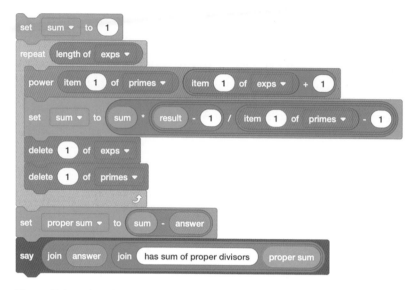

Figure 3-8: Using the exponents of n's prime factors to calculate the sum of n's divisors

We pull each prime p and its exponent k from the primes and exps lists and use our custom power block to calculate p^{k+1}. Then, we plug the results into the formula given earlier, keeping track of the total using the sum variable. When we reach the end of the two lists, we subtract the original number from sum before reporting the final answer. This gives us the sum of the number's *proper* divisors, excluding the number itself from the total.

Notice that both the primes and exps lists are cleared as the calculation proceeds. As with our program counting the number of divisors, it's easier to always grab the first item from each list and then delete that item, making the next list element the new element 1, rather than having to keep track of the item number within each list.

Hacking the Code

It's always a good idea to test your code as you write it to make sure it does what you want. For example, we can test our custom power block from Figure 3-7 by checking the box next to the result variable so its value appears on the stage. We can then drag the block into the programming area, enter values for the arguments, and click the block and see if result shows the correct value. Figure 3-9 tests the block by calculating flintmax. As we discussed in Chapter 1, this is the largest integer that Scratch Cat can get to when counting by ones.

result 9007199254740992

Figure 3-9: Calculating 2^{53}
using the power block

When I'm programming in Scratch, I debug my code by displaying lots of variables on the stage and isolating sections of the code to verify that it behaves as I expect. Once the code works, I clean up the stage by hiding the variables that don't need to be seen.

Programming Challenges

3.1   Remember that 6 is the first perfect number, so called because it's equal to the sum of its proper divisors: 1 + 2 + 3 = 6. Use the sum of divisors code in Figure 3-8 to find three other perfect numbers less than 10,000.

3.2   A number n can fail to be perfect in two ways: either the sum of proper divisors of n is less than n, in which case n is called *deficient*, or the sum of proper divisors of n is greater than n, in which case n is called *abundant*. Write some Scratch code that reports if a given number is deficient, perfect, or abundant. How many of each kind of number are there (up to 10, 100, 1,000)?

3.3   Raising a nonzero number to the 0 power gives an answer of 1. Check the exponent block in Figure 3-7 to see if it works for an exponent of 0. If it doesn't, rewrite the block so it gives the correct result.

3.4   Negative exponents are calculated using reciprocals: $n^{-k} = 1/n^k$. Make the exponent block give correct answers for negative exponents.

3.5   Change the code for τ and σ so that instead of deleting list elements after you access them you use a new counter variable, say i, to access each of the list elements in order.

How Prime Factorization Helps Find GCDs

In Chapter 2, we explored techniques for finding the greatest common divisor (GCD) of two integers b and a. If we know the prime factorization of each integer, we have another option. Say we have the following two prime factorizations:

$$a = 990 = 2^1 \cdot 3^2 \cdot 5^1 \cdot 11^1$$
$$b = 5{,}292 = 2^2 \cdot 3^3 \cdot 7^2$$

To find the GCD of b and a, the first step is to rewrite their prime factorizations to include each prime factor of either number, using exponent 0 if necessary:

$$a = 990 = 2^1 \cdot 3^2 \cdot 5^1 \cdot 7^0 \cdot 11^1$$
$$b = 5{,}292 = 2^2 \cdot 3^3 \cdot 5^0 \cdot 7^2 \cdot 11^0$$

Here, we've added 7^0 to the prime factorization of a and 5^0 and 11^0 to the prime factorization of b. Next, for each prime factor, we compare a and b and take the minimum exponent. For example, the minimum of 3^2 and 3^3 is 3^2. The GCD of b and a is the product of the prime factorization using just the minimum exponents:

$$GCD(b, a) = 2^1 \cdot 3^2 \cdot 5^0 \cdot 7^0 \cdot 11^0 = 2 \cdot 9 = 18$$

If we've already invested the time and effort to factor b and a, then this can be a useful approach. But if we don't know the factorizations ahead of time, it's more efficient to use Euclid's algorithm to find the GCD, as we did in Project 9.

A related concept to the GCD is the *least common multiple (LCM)*. The LCM of b and a is the smallest number that's a multiple of both. For example, the LCM of 2 and 3 is 6. The LCM is useful for adding fractions, since the LCM of the two denominators is the common denominator you should convert to before doing the addition. In this context, the least common multiple is called the *least common denominator (LCD)*. This can be a little confusing if you forget that the D in LCD stands for denominator while the D in GCD stands for divisor!

If we have the prime factorizations of b and a, calculating their LCM is quite similar to calculating their GCD. The only difference is that we take the *maximum* exponent of each prime factor rather than the minimum. Continuing with our example of $b = 5{,}292$ and $a = 990$, we get:

$$LCM(b, a) = 2^2 \cdot 3^3 \cdot 5^1 \cdot 7^2 \cdot 11^1$$
$$= 4 \cdot 27 \cdot 5 \cdot 49 \cdot 11$$
$$= 291{,}060$$

Since we use minimum exponents to find the GCD and maximum exponents to find the LCM, a neat hack is that multiplying the GCD and LCM of two numbers b and a is equivalent to multiplying the two numbers themselves:

$$GCD(b, a) \cdot LCM(b, a) = b \cdot a$$

By extension, if we've calculated $GCD(b, a)$, we can calculate $LCM(b, a)$ as:

$$LCM(b, a) = \frac{b \cdot a}{GCD(b, a)}$$

Programming Challenges

3.6 Write a custom block that will let you determine whether a given number is prime using trial division.

3.7 Use the block from Challenge 3.6 to write another custom block that will tell you the next prime number after a given number. If you wanted to program a GCD calculator using a factorization approach based on the program from Project 10 (Figure 3-3), you would need to make sure the lists of prime factors of the two numbers both had all the same primes, so blocks like these would come in handy.

3.8 A Spirograph is a classic toy that lets you draw intricate curves by rotating a toothed gear inside a toothed ring. The following picture shows how different gear sizes lead to different shapes. Lots of people have made Spirograph simulators using Scratch, and you can probably find other versions that run in web pages. Write a program to have Scratch Cat use GCD or LCM blocks to predict how many "points" a curve will have when a gear with b teeth is rotated inside a ring with 96 teeth.

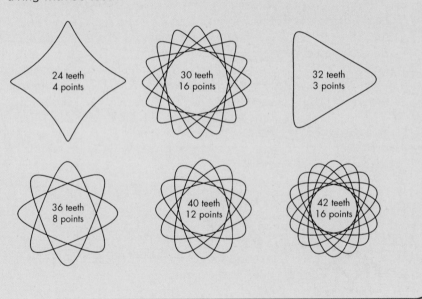

Contacting Aliens with Biprimes

Biprimes, also sometimes called *semiprimes*, are an intriguing group of numbers. As the product of two primes, a biprime by definition has just two prime factors. This opens up an interesting possibility: you can use the biprime to combine information from each of its prime factors.

Here's a real-life example where biprimes came in handy. In 1974, scientists broadcast the Arecibo message out into space from the Arecibo radio telescope in Puerto Rico. They wanted the message to include information about human life on Earth so that anyone who received it would know we exist and learn something about us. But they didn't want to write the message in English or some other human language, since the recipients might not understand it. Instead, the message's authors decided to design it as a series of bits (0s and 1s) meant to be arranged in a rectangle, with the 0 bits colored white and the 1 bits colored black, to produce a pixelated image. How long should the message be, though, and how would the receiver know to arrange the bits into a rectangle of the right size?

Imagine you're designing such a message. The message has n bits. If the rectangle has dimensions $a \cdot b$, you'll need to have a and b be factors of n, such that $a \cdot b = n$. If n were prime, there would be only one factorization, $1 \cdot n$ (or $n \cdot 1$), so the bits would be arranged in a single long row or column—pretty useless. But if n had lots of factors, there would be lots of possible dimensions for the rectangle—not very helpful either.

The solution is to make n a biprime. This way, it has only two significant factors (excluding 1 and n itself), the two primes that multiply together to make n, so the dimensions of the rectangle are clear. That's exactly what the Arecibo team did, sending a message of 1,679 bits. Since $1{,}679 = 73 \cdot 23$, there are only two possible ways to organize the bits: 23 rows and 73 columns, or 73 rows and 23 columns. For the bit string they sent, the first possibility decodes as a random arrangement of dots, but the second gives the image shown in Figure 3-10.

Figure 3-10: The Arecibo message

The message squeezes in information about counting in binary, the chemistry underlying life, the solar system, the size of a typical human, and the telescope that sent the message—pretty impressive for just 1,679 1s and 0s. Unfortunately, the Arecibo telescope collapsed in 2020, but even though the telescope is gone, the message is on its way to the globular cluster Messier 13 and should arrive in about 25,000 years.

To extract the information from the Arecibo message, all we need to do is factor its length, n. We already have a way to do that by trial division, as in Project 10, but this approach can be slow for large numbers—especially large biprimes—since we'll have to go through trial division with all the small numbers first. As we'll see in the next project, knowing that we're trying to factor a biprime gives us a shortcut. We might expect a biprime's two prime factors to be close to the same size, hovering around the square root of n. We can start looking from there instead of from 2.

Project 13: Fermat's Factorization Feat

The mathematician Pierre de Fermat realized that there's a more efficient way to factor numbers with two factors close to the same size, such as the biprimes we're interested in here. The technique is based on the formula for the difference of squares. Suppose we have the number n written as a difference of squares, $n = a^2 - b^2$. We can rewrite this as $n = (a - b)(a + b)$. Viewing the formula this way tells us that $(a - b)$ and $(a + b)$ must be factors of n.

The trick is to find a and b from n. For that, we'll rewrite the equation as $a^2 - n = b^2$, try various choices for a, and look for a choice that makes the difference $a^2 - n$ a perfect square, which we can use to find b. First, we need to recognize perfect squares, which we do in the custom block in Figure 3-11.

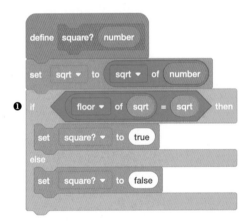

Figure 3-11: Do we have a perfect square?

This is a Boolean block, returning a logical value of true or false depending on whether the number passed in is a perfect square. We calculate the square root of number, use the built-in floor function to round the result down to the nearest integer ❶, and compare the two. If number is a perfect square, its square root is already an integer, so the comparison is equal.

Once we can recognize perfect squares, we can start searching for them to identify a and b and, by extension, the factors of n. The program in Figure 3-12 shows how.

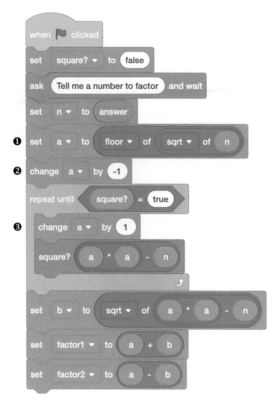

Figure 3-12: Fermat factorization

We start by picking a value of *a* just a little smaller than $\sqrt{n}$ ❶. Then, in a loop, we increase *a* by 1 ❸ and check if $a^2 - n$ is a perfect square. (Decreasing *a* by 1 just before the loop ❷ lets us catch the case where *n* happens to be a perfect square itself.) Once we've found a value of *b* that works, we calculate and display the factors factor1 (*a* + *b*) and factor2 (*a* – *b*).

The Results

Figure 3-13 shows the results of a sample run of the program.

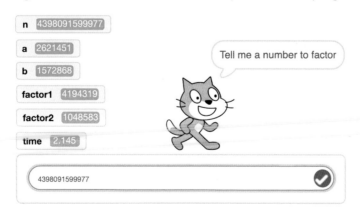

Figure 3-13: Factoring 4,398,091,599,977

Notice that rather than having Scratch Cat say the results, we simply display the relevant variables on the screen.

Hacking the Code

It would be interesting to compare the timing of the Fermat factorization approach to the trial division approach from Project 10. You might notice in Figure 3-13 that there's an extra variable showing on the screen, called time, for that purpose. We embedded a program in a timer loop before, in Project 9, when we were checking how long it took to test for a prime using trial division (see Figure 2-19 on page 39). This time, we'll create two simple custom blocks to turn Scratch's internal timer on and off, as shown in Figure 3-14.

Figure 3-14: Timer blocks

To time the Fermat factorization program, add the timer start block right before the third set block ❶ in Figure 3-12, and add the timer stop block to the end of the program. As we discussed in Chapter 2, Scratch's default time unit is seconds, so the time might be reported as 0 for small numbers because the actual time interval is too short to display after rounding. Running the program repeatedly and dividing the total time by the number of runs should give a more accurate result. This hack also helps cancel out the effect that other processes running on your computer have on the speed of the Scratch program.

Programming Challenges

3.9   Add a test to the Fermat factorization code in Figure 3-12 that checks whether the factors it produces are prime numbers. This will tell you if the input number is truly a biprime.

3.10   Combine the Fermat factorization code in Figure 3-12 with the trial division code from Figure 2-6 on page 28 so you can compare how long each method takes to find a factorization.

3.11 Scratch's stage is 480 pixels by 360 pixels. Write a program that takes a string of $n = a \cdot b$ bits (where a is at most 480 and b is at most 360) and displays it on the screen in a rectangle of a by b pixels, coloring in the 1 bits black and the 0 bits white. Try to use the program to re-create the Arecibo message.

Conclusion

We asked different questions in this chapter and in Chapter 2 ("How does a number factor?" and "Is a number prime?"), but we used the same initial approach to answer them in both cases: trial division. As we've seen, this approach is limited by the time we have available for performing the work. In the worst case, it takes as many steps as the square root of the number being tested to find an answer. For numbers up to flintmax, that isn't too long, but for numbers with hundreds of digits, there isn't enough time in the universe for trial division to work. Other approaches, such as Fermat factorization, can help us find the result we're looking for more quickly, especially when we have a clue about the shape of the number, such as whether it's a biprime. If you can think of a way to speed up the arithmetic, Scratch Cat will give you an answer more quickly!

4

Finding Patterns in Sequences

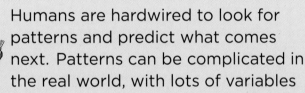Humans are hardwired to look for patterns and predict what comes next. Patterns can be complicated in the real world, with lots of variables and outcomes in time (when will the moon be full again?) or space (is there a bear in that cave?). In this chapter, we'll explore the patterns found in sequences of numbers. You'll learn how to uncover the rules for how a sequence is formed and how to predict later numbers in the sequence.

What Are Sequences?

A *sequence* is just a list of numbers. The numbers are listed in a particular order—there's a first number, a second number, a third number, and so on—so we can say that sequences are ordered, or *indexed*, by the positive integers. When we write about the mathematics of sequences, we often show the index numbers as subscripts. For example, we might write a sequence as $a_1, a_2, a_3, \ldots$, where each a is a value in the sequence, known as a *term* or an *element*.

Often, the numbers in a sequence tell a story about how they were generated. Maybe there's a rule that describes a formula for taking an index number and manipulating it to produce the corresponding element of the sequence. For example, if we wanted to study the sequence of odd numbers (1, 3, 5, 7, . . .), we might describe the nth odd number as $2n - 1$. We could arrive at this formula by thinking about the even numbers as multiples of 2 and odd numbers as 1 less than even numbers. We can do a quick check to make sure this works: the first odd number is when index $n = 1$, and $2 \cdot 1 - 1 = 1$. Next, when $n = 2$, we get $2n - 1 = 2 \cdot 2 - 1 = 3$, and so on. We can make the pattern explicit by saying $a_n = 2n - 1$, or, in words, *double the index and subtract one*.

Maybe each index n represents a mathematical object, like a geometric shape, and the corresponding number in the sequence can be found by examining or counting some feature of the object. For example, if we let each n represent a square of side length n, we might be interested in the sequence of the squares' areas (1, 4, 9, 16, . . .). Or maybe we'd want the sequence of the squares' perimeters instead (4, 8, 12, 16, . . .).

Finding the Next Value in a Sequence

It may be possible to find a formula for a sequence like the ones just described that's based on a geometric or logical pattern. That formula can then give us useful insight into what's going on with the sequence. For example, we might notice that the numbers in the area sequence are all perfect squares and recognize that this has to do with a square's area being a product of its length and width. Likewise, we might notice that the numbers in the perimeter sequence are all multiples of 4 and find a reason for this in a square's four equal sides. If we write the sequence of areas as $s_1, s_2, s_3, . . .$, and the sequence of perimeters as $p_1, p_2, p_3, . . .$, we might then find the formulas $s_n = n^2$ and $p_n = 4n$. These formulas are correct algebraically, but we arrived at them based on the geometric descriptions of the sequences.

Sometimes a sequence's pattern is best described by providing a recipe to produce later terms in the sequence based on earlier terms. A *recurrence* does this by giving a formula for a_n that's based not on the index n but on the values of previous elements. For example, the perimeter sequence could be generated by noting that $p_1 = 4$ and that each perimeter is 4 more than the previous one. The element before the element with index n has index $n - 1$, so the formula could be $p_n = p_{n-1} + 4$. As long as we have the starting value (which is p_1), we can generate the rest of the sequence.

The sequence of square areas also follows its own, more subtle recurrence. Given the starting element $s_1 = 1$, any later element s_n can be calculated as $s_{n-1} + 2n - 1$. This gives us another way to describe the sequence. In general, to specify a sequence by a recurrence you must provide an initial value (such as $p_1 = 4$) and a rule of formation (such as $p_n = p_{n-1} + 4$). Recurrences can sometimes depend on two or more preceding terms instead of just one, in which case two or more initial values must be given. A famous example is the Fibonacci sequence, which we'll explore soon.

Making Sequences in Scratch

In Scratch, we can represent sequences as lists. A Scratch list can hold numbers or strings and can be up to 200,000 items long, which is generous for exploring patterns. Unlike many other programming languages, which index list items starting from 0, Scratch indexes its lists starting from 1. This quirk makes Scratch lists especially useful for representing sequences, which are also typically indexed starting from 1. As mentioned in Chapter 3, when Scratch displays a list on the stage, it includes the index numbers down the left side, so you can easily see an item's position in the sequence. If the list is too long to fit on the stage, you can scroll down to see the later entries.

The Scratch blocks for working with lists are shown in Figure 4-1. These blocks are available in the Variables section of the block palette.

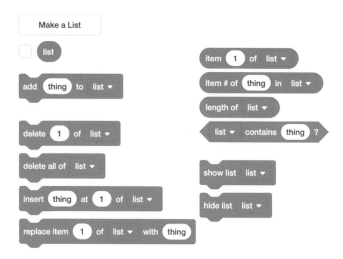

Figure 4-1: Scratch's list manipulation blocks

Notice that, as well as adding items at the end of a list, we can insert items at any position in the list, which causes the indices of later items to shift (increase) by 1. We can delete list items, which also shifts the later index numbers (reducing them by 1), and we can replace list items with other items, which leaves the later indices unchanged. We can look up an item's index to see where in the list it occurs, and we can check if an item occurs in the list at all. We can also see how long the list is.

Project 14: Fibonacci's Rabbits

In this project, we'll explore the *Fibonacci numbers*, a famous sequence described by a *two-term recurrence*. This means each number in the sequence is calculated based on the previous two. The sequence was first mentioned in western Europe in the book *Liber Abaci*, written by an Italian mathematician named Fibonacci in 1202. Fibonacci used the sequence to describe the growth of a population of rabbits.

After we're given the first two numbers in the Fibonacci sequence, $f_1 = 1$ and $f_2 = 1$, every other number is found using this rule of formation:

$$f_n = f_{n-1} + f_{n-2}$$

In other words, we add the two previous numbers in the sequence to get the next one. The third number is $1 + 1 = 2$, the fourth is $1 + 2 = 3$, the fifth is $2 + 3 = 5$, and so on. For more, we can let Scratch do the work, as in Figure 4-2.

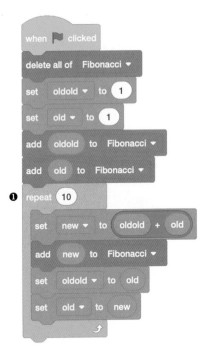

Figure 4-2: Generating the Fibonacci sequence using a two-term recurrence

Notice in this code that to generate numbers in a two-term recurrence, we need to keep track of only the previous two values to calculate the next one. We first set the variables named oldold and old to the starting values (1 and 1). Then, in a loop ❶, we assign the new variable their sum, replace oldold with old, and replace old with new. With these replacements, we're ready to calculate the next value of new the next time through the loop.

Project 15: The Golden Ratio

An interesting fact about the Fibonacci sequence is that the ratios of successive numbers approach a limiting value, meaning the value of f_n divided by f_{n-1} gets closer and closer to a particular number (the *limit*) as the sequence goes on, without ever quite reaching it. This is known as a *convergent ratio*. For Fibonacci numbers, the limit is a famous mathematical constant called the *golden ratio*. Its exact value is:

$$\frac{1 + \sqrt{5}}{2} \approx 1.618034$$

To prove that the Fibonacci numbers have a convergent ratio, we can modify the code from the previous project, adding another list that keeps track of the ratios of each number with the previous number in the sequence. Figure 4-3 shows how.

Figure 4-3: Tracking the ratios of successive Fibonacci terms

The code is similar to Figure 4-2, but with an extra list to keep track of the Fibonacci ratio. We update this list with the value of old / oldold before calculating the next term in the sequence ❷. We let the list go through 40 iterations ❶ because that's where the value of the ratio stabilizes.

The Results

Figure 4-4 shows the initial results in the two lists after running the code shown in Figure 4-3. You'll have to scroll down to see the later values in the lists.

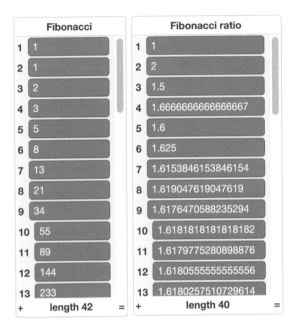

Fibonacci		Fibonacci ratio	
1	1	1	1
2	1	2	2
3	2	3	1.5
4	3	4	1.6666666666666667
5	5	5	1.6
6	8	6	1.625
7	13	7	1.6153846153846154
8	21	8	1.619047619047619
9	34	9	1.6176470588235294
10	55	10	1.6181818181818182
11	89	11	1.6179775280898876
12	144	12	1.6180555555555556
13	233	13	1.6180257510729614
+	length 42 =	+	length 40 =

Figure 4-4: The first Fibonacci numbers and their ratios

The Fibonacci list shows the Fibonacci sequence itself, while the Fibonacci ratio list shows the ratio between each term and the one that follows it. As you can see, the ratios bounce around above and below their limiting value. If you wanted to stop the program early, taking the average of two successive list elements in Fibonacci ratio would give a better approximation of the limiting value than either element alone.

Hacking the Code

We used a repeat loop to give the program what seemed like a reasonable number of terms to calculate, but it may be better to let it decide for itself how many terms it needs. For instance, we could have the program stop calculating Fibonacci numbers when the ratios have sufficiently converged to the limiting value. We could define this as the point when the ratio values are no longer changing, or when they change by less than a specified amount. Figure 4-5 shows a modified Fibonacci program that uses this approach.

This program no longer stores the Fibonacci numbers in a list, since we're interested only in how long it takes for the ratios to converge. We use a repeat until loop ❶ to monitor the ratios as more terms are calculated, stopping when the difference between the current and previous ratio is less than 0.0000001. This accuracy level is configurable, but if we use too many digits (too small a number), we'll run into the limitations of the IEEE 754 floating-point representation.

Notice that the repeat until condition uses an absolute value function (abs). This is necessary because the ratios seesaw around the limiting value, alternately too big and too small. This means the difference we calculate is alternately positive and negative, so abs converts the negative values to positive.

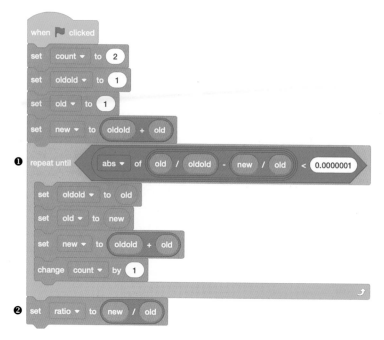

Figure 4-5: Stopping the program when the ratio converges

The program includes a variable called count to keep track of how many terms we need to get to the specified accuracy level. After the loop ends, the program stores the final ratio in the ratio variable ❷. On the stage, only the first few digits of the ratio are shown, but you can click the ratio in the coding area to see all the digits that were calculated, as shown in Figure 4-6.

Figure 4-6: Calculating the Fibonacci ratio

As an experiment, you might try setting the accuracy level to different values (0.01, 0.001, . . .) to see how many terms it takes to reach that level of accuracy.

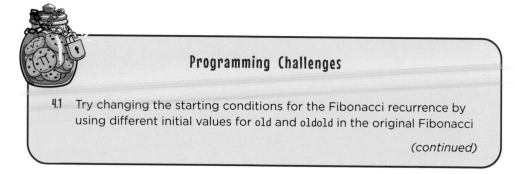

Programming Challenges

4.1 Try changing the starting conditions for the Fibonacci recurrence by using different initial values for old and oldold in the original Fibonacci

(continued)

program (Figure 4-2). Setting old to 2 and oldold to 1 wouldn't be very interesting, since that just gives the Fibonacci sequence shifted by one number. Setting old to 1 and oldold to 2, however, gives a different sequence, called the *Lucas sequence*. See if you can find any relationships between Lucas numbers and Fibonacci numbers.

4.2 How could you make sense of Fibonacci numbers going backward? What should f_0 be to preserve the recurrence? How about f_{-1} and f_{-2}? Program a recurrence for negative integers.

4.3 Play with the code in Figure 4-2 to explore its limits. How far can the Fibonacci sequence go before the numbers it generates exceed flintmax? How far before the numbers exceed the absolute limit for Scratch's floating-point representation and are reported as Infinity? The rate of growth is exponential, so it doesn't take many steps before flintmax is exceeded!

Figurate Numbers

Figurate numbers come from sequences that count how many points it takes to build nested geometric figures. For example, in Figure 4-7 we have squares that fit ("nest") inside one another. The blue points are the points we want to count, in this case positioned on a grid. By drawing connections between the points, starting from the bottom-left corner, we can create increasingly larger squares that encompass more and more of the points.

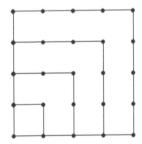

Figure 4-7: Nested squares as figurate numbers

The word *square* can be a noun or a verb. As a noun, it names a geometric object, a polygon with four equal sides and four equal angles. As a verb, it's more often used for arithmetic, to describe the process of multiplying a number by itself. Of course, the arithmetic and geometry are related. The formula $A = s^2$, used to calculate the area of a (geometric) square by multiplying the length of a side s by itself, interprets the arithmetic in a geometrical way. Numbers are squares if they're the result of multiplying a positive integer by itself ($1^2 = 1$, $2^2 = 4$, $3^2 = 9$, 16, 25, ...).

Figure 4-7 shows how we can arrange square numbers of points to form ever-growing geometric squares. We have a square with 4 points (2 rows of 2) inside a square with 9 points (3 rows of 3) inside a square with 16 points (4 rows of 4) inside a square with 25 points (5 rows of 5). You can think of the bottom-left point itself as a square with 1 point, too. Each larger square adds a new set of connected points around the edges of the previous square.

In fact, any kind of polygon can be nested to make a sequence of figurate numbers like the sequence of squares, as we'll explore next.

Project 16: Square, Triangular, and Pentagonal Numbers?

The Scratch program in the next three figures draws nested *s*-sided polygons and counts the newly added points around the edges to generate a sequence. So far, we haven't used many of Scratch's graphics capabilities, but in this program we use the Pen extension to animate the drawing of various figures. (Click the **Add Extensions** icon in the bottom-left corner to add these Pen blocks.) Our program starts with the initial setup in Figure 4-8.

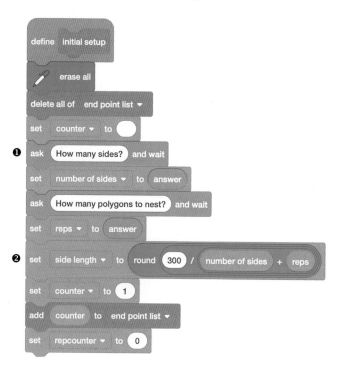

Figure 4-8: The setup code for drawing nested polygons

This `initial` setup block erases previous drawings from the screen and asks the user for the number of sides (in the variable `number of sides`) and the number of polygons to nest (in the variable `reps`) ❶. The calculation of `side length` ❷, which is the distance on the stage between two adjacent points, makes sure the polygons will fit on the stage.

Figure 4-9 shows the main logic of the program.

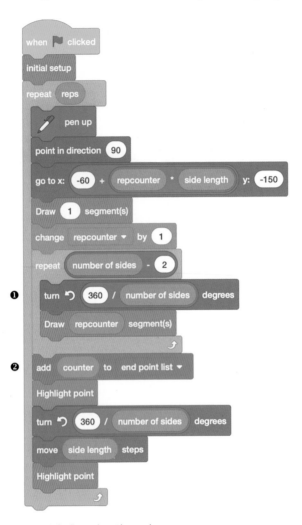

Figure 4-9: Drawing the polygons

We draw the nested polygons in a loop that repeats reps times. We start drawing each polygon from the bottom-left corner, using the go to block to skip any dots that we've already drawn (since the polygons all share the same base). After drawing the first side with a custom Draw n segment(s) block, we rotate the pen ❶ depending on the number of sides of the polygon. The counter variable keeps track of the total number of points drawn. Once the current polygon is complete, we add counter to end point list ❷. This list keeps track of how many points we've drawn at the end of each completed polygon, building up our figurate number sequence. We use a custom Highlight point block to specify how the points are drawn. Figure 4-10 shows these two custom blocks.

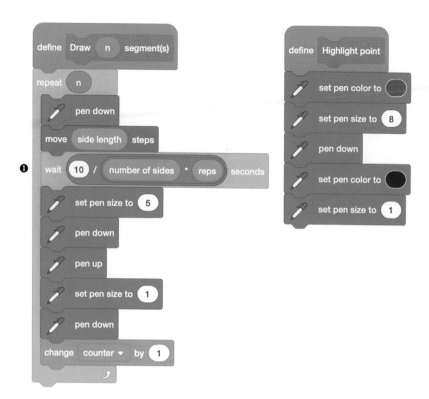

Figure 4-10: Drawing points and lines

The Draw n segment(s) block takes n steps along the side of a polygon, first drawing a large dot (pen size 5) and then drawing a thin line (pen size 1) to connect with the next dot. The wait block calculates a pause between each step ❶, but if you get tired of watching the drawing happen, you can speed it up by lowering the value in the numerator.

The custom Highlight point block simply changes the pen color to red and increases its size to mark the final dot in each polygon. Then, it changes the pen color back to blue and reduces the size again.

The Results

Let's use the drawing program to generate some sequences. For the number of sides $s = 4$ we get squares, both geometrically and arithmetically, as shown in Figure 4-11. Geometrically, each added layer of dots around the existing ones forms a new, larger square. Arithmetically, the numbers accumulated in the end point list sequence are all perfect squares. We arrived at these numbers by counting points, starting from the lower-left corner and moving counterclockwise, expanding outward with each layer of nesting. As mentioned earlier, when we complete a square, the number of points counted so far is added to the list and the point is highlighted in red.

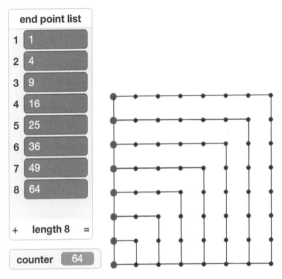

Figure 4-11: Square figurate numbers

There's no need to restrict ourselves to squares. *Triangular numbers* are the sequence generated by arranging points in nested equilateral triangles, as shown in Figure 4-12.

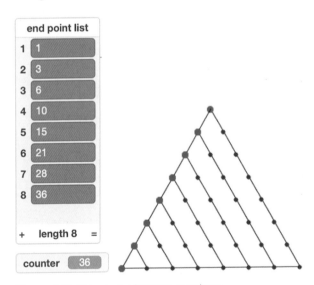

Figure 4-12: Triangular figurate numbers

Notice that each triangular number is built by adding the next integer to the triangular number that came before: 1, 1 + 2 = 3, 1 + 2 + 3 = 6, 1 + 2 + 3 + 4 = 10, and so on. In other words, the nth triangular number is the sum of all the integers from 1 to n.

How can we describe the pattern of the sequence of triangular numbers with a formula? Think about putting a copy of the nth triangle next to itself, rotated to make a parallelogram, as shown in Figure 4-13.

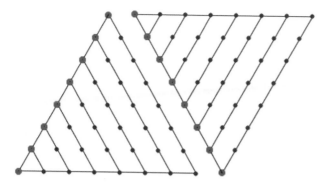

Figure 4-13: We can make a formula for triangular numbers by thinking about two triangles arranged to make a parallelogram.

The parallelogram has $n + 1$ dots across the bottom and n rows of dots, so there are $n(n + 1)$ dots in all. Since the parallelogram was made with two copies of the triangle, each triangle has $n(n + 1) / 2$ dots in it. There's the formula for the nth triangular number.

We can make another sequence of figurate numbers, which will be of use in Chapter 7, by counting points in nested pentagons. Figure 4-14 shows the sequence of *pentagonal numbers*.

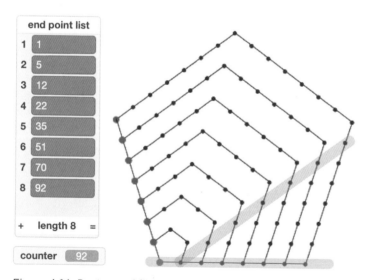

end point list	
1	1
2	5
3	12
4	22
5	35
6	51
7	70
8	92
+	length 8 =
counter	92

Figure 4-14: Pentagonal figurate numbers

There are other interesting sequences hidden in the nested pentagons. For example, if you count the points and write down just the numbers of those along the green path in Figure 4-14, you get 1, 2, 6, 13, 23, 36,..., as the sequence. Another path that gives a sequence we'll need in Chapter 7 starts at 2 and goes up and to the right, along the purple path in Figure 4-14. Counting around the nested pentagons gives the numbers 2, 7, 15, 26, 40, 57,..., as the sequence.

Hacking the Code

Even if you set the wait time in the Draw n segment(s) block (Figure 4-10 ❶) to 0, there's still a delay in drawing the polygons and reporting the values of the sequence of figurate numbers. If you want the results right away, you can speed up the program by using Turbo Mode (see Figure 4-15).

Figure 4-15: Turning on Turbo Mode

Turbo Mode is a feature that eliminates the short pause that Scratch usually inserts after running blocks that update the screen. To turn it on, select **Edit ▶ Turn on Turbo Mode** in the Scratch Editor or hold down SHIFT while clicking the green flag button. When Turbo Mode is activated, there's an indication in the menu bar.

Predicting Values in a Sequence

Whenever you see the first few terms in a sequence, a natural question is "What comes next?" One possible answer is "Whatever you want!" If all you know is that there are some numbers listed one after the other, then any number can come next. But if you assume that the numbers mean something—that they're generated by following some kind of rule—then figuring out what comes next requires discovering the rule and applying it to generate the later terms. There may be more than one rule that works, in which case you can pick the one that seems most natural or useful to you.

For example, consider the sequence of square numbers in Figure 4-11. We could predict the next number in the sequence by finding the rule that the nth element in the sequence is n^2. The element after $9^2 = 81$ should, then, be $10^2 = 100$. Alternatively, we could notice that for each new (geometric) square, we're building on the squares that came before by adding another shell of dots along the top and right sides. The nth shell adds the nth odd number ($2n - 1$) of points to the total (so the sequence could be described as $1, 1 + 3, 1 + 3 + 5, 1 + 3 + 5 + 7, \ldots$). This is an example of an *addition rule*, and it highlights a different aspect of the pattern. Thinking this way, we would get from the ninth number in the sequence (81) to the tenth number by adding $(2 \cdot 10) - 1 = 19$, giving us $81 + 19 = 100$. Either way, we make the same prediction, but we describe what's going on differently.

Project 17: Difference Tables Make All the Difference

One way to understand the pattern in a sequence built with some sort of addition rule is to undo the addition by doing a subtraction. A *difference table* for a sequence is another sequence built by subtracting each term of the original sequence from the next one. In this project, we'll explore how to use Scratch to create difference tables.

If one difference table isn't enough to reveal a sequence's pattern, we can create a second difference table by finding the differences between adjacent numbers in the first difference table. These are known as the *second differences* of the original sequence. If necessary, we can then make a third difference table based on the second, and so on. Sometimes, interesting patterns emerge from this process.

Figure 4-16 shows some Scratch code to take in a sequence and generate its difference table.

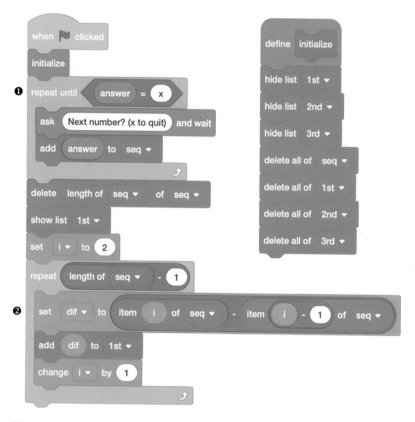

Figure 4-16: Building a difference table to analyze a sequence

First, the `initialize` block clears out the data from the last time the program was run. Then, the `repeat until` loop ❶ prompts us to enter a sequence, one number at a time, until we let Scratch know we're done by entering an x. The sequence is stored in the seq list. We then build the first difference table in the 1st list by calculating the differences between adjacent values in the sequence ❷.

The additional code in Figure 4-17 finds the second and third differences, storing them in the 2nd and 3rd lists.

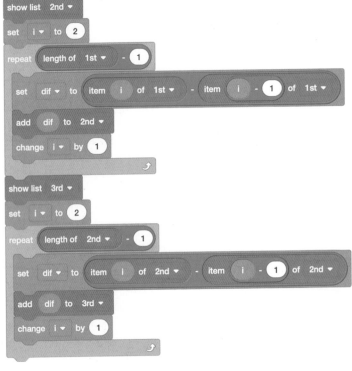

Figure 4-17: Calculating the second and third differences

This code segment follows the same pattern we used to calculate the first difference table, except we use the 1st and 2nd lists as input instead of using seq.

The Results

Figure 4-18 shows the result of running the difference table program for the first several values from the sequence of squares: 1, 4, 9, 16, 25, 36, 49, 64, and 81.

	seq		1st		2nd		3rd
1	1	1	3	1	2	1	0
2	4	2	5	2	2	2	0
3	9	3	7	3	2	3	0
4	16	4	9	4	2	4	0
5	25	5	11	5	2	5	0
6	36	6	13	6	2	6	0
7	49	7	15	7	2		
8	64	8	17				
9	81						
+	length 9 =	+	length 8 =	+	length 7 =	+	length 6 =

Figure 4-18: Difference tables for the sequence of squares

The first difference table confirms what we discussed earlier: the differences are successive odd numbers, meaning the nth number in the sequence is the sum of the first n odd numbers. The second differences are constant: they're all equal to 2, since successive odd numbers are always 2 apart. The third differences are all 0.

Third differences of 0 are a dead giveaway that the sequence's underlying rule of formation can be given as a *quadratic polynomial*, an expression of the form $ax^2 + bx + c$. Writing the rule of formation then becomes a matter of determining the values of a, b, and c, known as *coefficients*. For the sequence of square numbers, it's especially easy to write the quadratic polynomial: we can use $a = 1$, $b = 0$, and $c = 0$. This gives us:

$$1x^2 + 0x + 0 = x^2$$

For the triangular numbers from Figure 4-13, we can use $a = 1/2$, $b = 1/2$, and $c = 0$. Then we get:

$$\frac{1}{2}x^2 + \frac{1}{2}x + 0 = \frac{x^2 + x}{2} = \frac{x(x+1)}{2}$$

This is the same rule we arrived at before by treating two copies of the triangle as a parallelogram.

Hacking the Code

Here's a Scratch trick to make programs with lists easier to use. Suppose you have a list of numbers from another program—for example, the pentagonal numbers you generated with the code from Project 16 (Figure 4-14)—and you want to bring them into your difference table program for analysis. Rather than copying over the numbers by hand, one by one, you can export the whole list from that project by right-clicking it and selecting **Export** (see Figure 4-19). This will save the list as a text file called *end point list.txt* (or whatever the name of the list is) in your default directory.

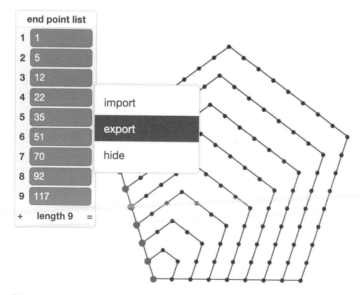

Figure 4-19: Saving a list for later use

To use that list in the difference table program, ignore the prompt to enter a number and instead right-click the seq list on the stage. Click **Import**, as shown in Figure 4-20, and select the file you just saved to upload it.

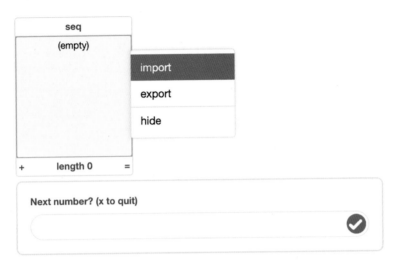

Figure 4-20: Recovering a list for further work

The seq list will now be populated with the pentagonal numbers, so you need to enter only an x into the prompt to have the differences calculated. Figure 4-21 shows the results.

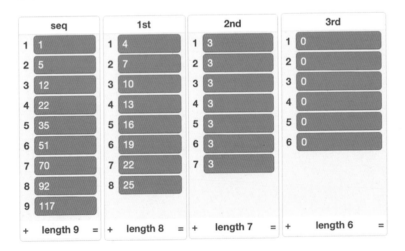

Figure 4-21: Difference tables for the sequence of pentagonal numbers

What do you know? Again, the third differences are all 0, so the sequence of pentagonal numbers can be generated using a quadratic polynomial too!

Programming Challenges

4.4 Write a Scratch program that takes any sequence with third differences of 0 and recovers the coefficients *a*, *b*, and *c* for that sequence's quadratic polynomial, $ax^2 + bx + c$. Use the program to find the coefficients for the pentagonal numbers. If all you want is the pentagonal number formula, it might help to draw the *n*th pentagon the way a young child draws a house, as a square with a triangular roof on top, and see it as the *n*th square with the (*n* − 1)st triangle on top.

4.5 If you exported the list of primes generated by the sieving program from Project 7, import it into the difference table program and see what happens. The first few results are shown here. As you can see, there isn't such a neat pattern of differences. Write some code to find the largest difference in the table of first differences.

seq	1st	2nd	3rd
1 2	1 1	1 1	1 -1
2 3	2 2	2 0	2 2
3 5	3 2	3 2	3 -4
4 7	4 4	4 -2	4 4
5 11	5 2	5 2	5 -4
6 13	6 4	6 -2	6 4
7 17	7 2	7 2	7 0
8 19	8 4	8 2	8 -6
9 23	9 6	9 -4	9 8
10 29	10 2	10 4	10 -6
11 31	11 6	11 -2	11 0
12 37	12 4	12 -2	12 4
13 41	13 2	13 2	13 0
+ length 17984 =	+ length 17983 =	+ length 17982 =	+ length 17981 =

4.6 Generate a sequence with this rule: the *n*th term of the sequence is the number of occurrences of the digit 1 in the binary representation of *n*. This sequence starts 1, 1, 2, 1, 2, 2, 3, ..., (from counting 1s in the binary sequence 1, 10, 11, 100, 101, 110, 111, ...). Write a Scratch program to calculate a few hundred terms of this sequence and see if you can find either a formula or a recurrence relation to predict future terms.

(continued)

4.7 What happens when you make a difference table of the Fibonacci sequence?

4.8 What happens when you make a difference table of the sequence of powers of 2?

4.9 Try creating a difference table of the sequence of cubes (1, 8, 27, 64, 125,...). You can extend the code from Figure 4-17 to get higher differences to explore difference tables for higher-degree polynomials.

Conclusion

Lists in Scratch are great for keeping track of sequences of numbers, and list arithmetic helps us make sense of the patterns that show up. Scratch graphics use geometry to animate sequences of figurate numbers, and difference tables make the patterns in these sequences easier to see. Scratch Cat has all the answers—your job is to ask the questions!

5

From Sequences to Arrays

When you ask, "What value comes next?" you're making an assumption that the values are arranged in one dimension, along a line. One value follows another in a sequence, such that there's only one way to step from one item to the next. But we live in a world with more than one dimension, and it's sometimes helpful to use more than one dimension to organize information.

For example, an *array* is a two-dimensional object, a table of values organized in rows and columns. We can still look for patterns in an array of numbers, but now the patterns might show up as we move from row to row, from column to column, or along diagonals. In this chapter, we'll use Scratch to study some interesting arrays. While Scratch makes it easy to explore one-dimensional sequences with its list data type, it doesn't have a similar structure for two-dimensional arrays. We'll have to develop some creative workarounds to represent arrays in Scratch.

Pascal's Triangle

Pascal's triangle is a two-dimensional array of numbers, rather than a linear sequence. Just as a sequence has entries indexed by the positive integers, entries in Pascal's triangle are specified by giving two index numbers, corresponding to the row and column numbers for a particular entry. In this case, it's best to think of the index numbers as starting from 0 rather than 1.

The row numbers in Pascal's triangle are represented with the letter n. For the first row, $n = 0$, for the second row, $n = 1$, and so on. Within each row, columns are represented with the letter k, beginning with $k = 0$ and continuing up to $k = n$. So the nth row always has $n + 1$ entries: row 0 has one entry, row 1 has two entries, and so on. Centering the rows when we write them out makes it easy to see how the array expands from one row to the next, giving Pascal's triangle its distinctive shape:

```
            1
         1     1
      1     2     1
    1    3     3    1
  1    4    6     4    1
1    5   10    10    5    1
            ⋮
```

The values of each entry can be determined by adding the two entries immediately above it. For example, the 2 in row $n = 2$ (the third row from the top) is the sum of the two 1s in the row above it, and each 10 in row $n = 5$ (the bottom row shown here) is the sum of the 4 and 6 above it. The entries at the edges of the rows, which don't have two entries above them, are all given a value of 1.

Working with Binomials

Now you know where the values in Pascal's triangle come from, but what do they mean? They relate to the *binomial theorem*. This algebraic rule makes it easier to work out the positive integer powers of *binomials*, expressions that are a sum of two terms. Taking $1 + x$ as an example binomial, the binomial theorem helps us calculate the value of $(1 + x)^0$, $(1 + x)^1$, $(1 + x)^2$, $(1 + x)^3$, and so on. Expanding each of these powers, we get the following:

$$(1 + x)^0 = 1$$
$$(1 + x)^1 = 1 + x$$
$$(1 + x)^2 = 1 + 2x + x^2$$
$$(1 + x)^3 = 1 + 3x + 3x^2 + x^3$$
$$(1 + x)^4 = 1 + 4x + 6x^2 + 4x^3 + x^4$$
$$(1 + x)^5 = 1 + 5x + 10x^2 + 10x^3 + 5x^4 + x^5$$

$$\vdots$$

Look familiar? The coefficients (the constant multipliers of powers of x) in these expansions are the same as the values in Pascal's triangle. The 1 in the first row of the triangle (row $n = 0$) corresponds to $(1 + x)^0 = 1$. The two 1s in the second row ($n = 1$) correspond to $(1 + x)^1 = 1 + x$. (Imagine an invisible 1 in front of the x.) The 1, 2, and 1 in the third row ($n = 2$) correspond to $(1 + x)^2 = 1 + 2x + x^2$, and so on.

In general, the nth row of Pascal's triangle shows the coefficients for the nth power of a binomial—that is, $(1 + x)^n$. What's more, the kth entry in that row holds the coefficient of x^k in the binomial's expansion. To see that, it helps to recognize that an expression such as $1 + 2x + x^2$ is equivalent to the expression $1x^0 + 2x^1 + 1x^2$ and to notice how the exponents of x count up from 0 to n.

Since the values in Pascal's triangle represent the coefficients in binomial expansions, they're known as *binomial coefficients*. Any given binomial coefficient can be written as $C(n, k)$, where again n and k are the row and column numbers in Pascal's triangle. So we can write Pascal's triangle symbolically like this:

$$C(0, 0)$$
$$C(1, 0) \quad C(1, 1)$$
$$C(2, 0) \quad C(2, 1) \quad C(2, 2)$$
$$C(3, 0) \quad C(3, 1) \quad C(3, 2) \quad C(3, 3)$$
$$C(4, 0) \quad C(4, 1) \quad C(4, 2) \quad C(4, 3) \quad C(4, 4)$$
$$C(5, 0) \quad C(5, 1) \quad C(5, 2) \quad C(5, 3) \quad C(5, 4) \quad C(5, 5)$$
$$\vdots$$

We've represented Pascal's triangle as a triangular array. But if you look at the pattern of index numbers, it makes just as much sense to see it as a square array, with the upper-right portion of the square either left off or filled with 0s, as shown here:

$C(0, 0)$	0	0	0	0	0
$C(1, 0)$	$C(1, 1)$	0	0	0	0
$C(2, 0)$	$C(2, 1)$	$C(2, 2)$	0	0	0
$C(3, 0)$	$C(3, 1)$	$C(3, 2)$	$C(3, 3)$	0	0
$C(4, 0)$	$C(4, 1)$	$C(4, 2)$	$C(4, 3)$	$C(4, 4)$	0
$C(5, 0)$	$C(5, 1)$	$C(5, 2)$	$C(5, 3)$	$C(5, 4)$	$C(5, 5)$

$$\vdots$$

We could find values for $C(n, k)$ by algebra, multiplying out the polynomials $(1 + x)^n$ to see what the coefficients turn out to be. (I've already done some of that for you, showing you the values up to $n = 5$.) But that would be a lot of work. To get a more general formula for $C(n, k)$, it helps to interpret the algebra by thinking about a related counting problem.

Making Subsets from Sets

Suppose you have five friends (Albert, Barb, Charley, Deb, and Eve), and you can invite only three of them to come over for pizza. How many different sets of three people could you invite? Let ABC be *Albert, Barb, Charley*, the first possibility. BAC is the same set of people in a different order, so this shouldn't really count as different; you'll still have the same guests at your pizza party. ABD is a different set, though, and so is ABE. You can keep going, one subset at a time, and eventually list 10 different pizza party sets, maybe ending with CDE.

How can you confirm that number is correct? Let's see if we can formulate a general rule. Suppose you have a set with n objects in it (all your friends), and you want to build a subset with k objects in it (the party guests), for some integer k where $0 \leq k \leq n$. In our example, $n = 5$ and $k = 3$. First, think about the situation where the order of the elements selected for the subset *does* matter. In that case, the first element can be any of the n elements in the set. The second element can be any of the $n - 1$ elements left over after the first one is chosen, the third element can be any of the remaining $n - 2$ elements, and so on, until we arrive at the kth element, which can be chosen only in $n - (k - 1) = n - k + 1$ ways. In our example, we pick any of our five friends (A through E) for the first choice, then any of the four left after that for the second choice, and then any of the three remaining people for the third choice.

Multiplying the number of available choices for each spot gives us the total number of possible combinations. In the case of $k = 3$ spots for $n = 5$ friends, there are $5 \cdot 4 \cdot 3 = 60$ possibilities. In general, the formula for the number of possible combinations is:

$$n \cdot (n - 1) \cdot (n - 2) \cdot \ldots \cdot (n - k + 1)$$

In our example, though, the order of the elements selected for the subset doesn't matter, so we have to deal with the fact that different orderings of the k choices can lead to the same subset (like the ABC and BAC orderings mentioned earlier). How can we figure out how many different ways there are to order a subset of k elements? We can apply the same logic we just used for n to find out: there are k possibilities for what the first element could be, then $k - 1$ possibilities for the second element, and so on. So the total number of orderings is:

$$(k - 0) \cdot (k - 1) \cdot (k - 2) \cdot \ldots \cdot 1$$

For $k = 3$, for example, there are $3 \cdot 2 \cdot 1 = 6$ ways to order a particular set of three elements. This means that if we want to count only the unique subsets, ignoring rearrangements, we should count only one out of every six of the total number of combinations. That is, if there are $5 \cdot 4 \cdot 3$ ways to pick three elements from a group of five, and there are $3 \cdot 2 \cdot 1$ ways to order those three elements, there are $(5 \cdot 4 \cdot 3) / (3 \cdot 2 \cdot 1) = 60 / 6 = 10$ unique subsets, ignoring order. The general formula is:

$$\frac{n \cdot (n - 1) \cdot (n - 2) \cdot \ldots \cdot (n - k + 1)}{k \cdot (k - 1) \cdot (k - 2) \cdot \ldots \cdot 1}$$

Notice that we've been using the same variables here that we were using to identify the rows and columns in Pascal's triangle: n and k. That's because the two problems are related. The formula to calculate a particular term $C(n, k)$ in Pascal's triangle—and, by extension, the formula to determine a particular binomial coefficient—is the same one we just worked out:

$$C(n, k) = \frac{n \cdot (n-1) \cdot (n-2) \cdot \ldots \cdot (n-k+1)}{k \cdot (k-1) \cdot (k-2) \cdot \ldots \cdot 1}$$

There's a special sequence, the *factorial numbers*, that lets us write the formula for $C(n, k)$ in a neater way. If n is a positive integer, n factorial (written as $n!$) is the product of every integer from 1 to n. For example, 3! is $1 \cdot 2 \cdot 3 = 6$, and 5! is $1 \cdot 2 \cdot 3 \cdot 4 \cdot 5 = 120$. More formally:

$$n! = n \cdot (n-1) \cdot (n-2) \cdot \ldots \cdot 2 \cdot 1$$

Looking at the sequences of terms in the formula for $C(n, k)$, it's clear there's some kind of factorial logic involved. With a bit of algebra, we can simplify the formula to make factorial notation apply:

$$C(n, k) = \frac{n!}{k!(n-k)!}$$

Calculating factorials manually gets tedious as n and k get bigger. With Scratch Cat's help, however, it's a breeze.

Project 18: Pick a Number from Pascal's Triangle

In this project, we'll use the factorial definition we just arrived at for $C(n, k)$ to make Scratch calculate the binomial coefficient for any given values of n and k. Put another way, we'll write a program that calculates the entry at the nth row and kth column of Pascal's triangle. Figure 5-1 shows how.

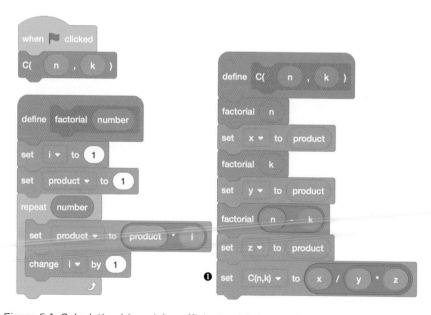

Figure 5-1: Calculating binomial coefficients with factorials

The main program is the shortest one in this book: it's just one line, to call the custom block that calculates the binomial coefficient for a given n and k. That block, in turn, calls the factorial calculator block, which takes in a value and calculates its factorial, using a loop to multiply all the numbers from 1 up to that value. The result is held in the product variable, which we set to 1 at the start of the block.

We use the factorial block three times to calculate n factorial, k factorial, and n - k factorial, storing the resulting values of product in the variables x, y, and z. Then, we calculate x / y * z to get the binomial coefficient ❶. This is the equivalent of our formula:

$$C(n, k) = \frac{n!}{k!(n-k)!}$$

This program uses sliders to set the n and k inputs. Sliders are more efficient at receiving input than the ask and wait block in previous projects, and they let us automatically limit the input values to only integers within a certain range, sparing us from having to screen for inappropriate inputs like negative integers, strings, or numbers with decimals. To create a slider for a variable, right-click the variable on the stage and choose **slider** from the drop-down menu, as in Figure 5-2.

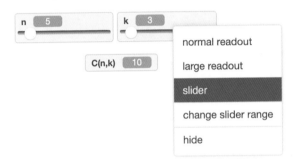

Figure 5-2: Using sliders to calculate C(5, 3) = 10

Dragging the slider's circle to the left or right changes the associated variable's value over a range you can specify using the change slider range option from the drop-down menu. I set the slider ranges to be 1 to 50 for *n* and 0 to 50 for *k*, but as we'll discuss, even those ranges might cause trouble for some of the binomial coefficients we calculate.

To use the program, set the sliders to your chosen *n* and *k* values, then click the green flag to see the resulting binomial coefficient.

Hacking the Code

There's a problem with this program. I set up the pizza party counting scenario with the assumption that *k* (the number of guests allowed) is less than or equal to *n* (the total number of people to choose from). But while the sliders limit *n* and *k* to integers, there's nothing stopping us from making *k* greater than *n*.

If we set the sliders this way, when it comes time to calculate (*n* - *k*)!, we'll end up passing the factorial block a negative number. A repeat loop can't repeat a negative number of times, so the loop will exit before the first pass and product will be stuck with its initial value of 1. This breaks the formula and reports a weird result, as shown in Figure 5-3.

C(n,k) 0.166667

Figure 5-3: C(5, 6) = ???

The fix is pretty easy: just put a test into the main program to check for $k > n$ and notify the user that the inputs are invalid if this condition is met, as shown in Figure 5-4.

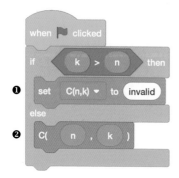

Figure 5-4: Adding a check for k > n

Notice that we're using a variable called C(n,k) ❶, while also using a custom block called C with n and k inputs ❷ to calculate a value to assign to that variable. Scratch's color coding and block shapes help us keep track of which C(n, k) is which.

Another problem with this program is that factorials get big quickly: 18! is the largest factorial Scratch can reliably calculate before reaching flintmax. In practice, since $n!$ is always divisible by various powers of 2, the reported value remains correct for a while even after exceeding flintmax, but by the time we get to 171! we've exceeded the overall maximum of the IEEE 754 floating-point standard. At that point, Scratch gives up, reporting values involving calculations of 171! or larger as Infinity (see Figure 5-5).

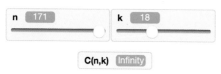

C(n,k) Infinity

Figure 5-5: C(171, 18) = ???

Even for smaller values, the rounding in IEEE 754 for integers larger than flintmax can spoil the results and yield a non-integer value, as shown in Figure 5-6.

C(n,k) 58343356817423.984

Figure 5-6: C(49, 23) = ???

In fairness, the true value of $C(49, 23)$ is 58,343,356,817,424, so Scratch is pretty close, but "pretty close" isn't good enough. To enable Scratch to keep finding the exact binomial coefficients for bigger values of n and k, we need to take a different approach, one that doesn't involve working with factorials. For this, we can take advantage of the fact that even though the factorials in the formula for $C(n, k)$ quickly get large, the binomial coefficients themselves don't grow so big so fast. So if we can calculate the binomial coefficients without first calculating any factorials, we'll be able to get a lot further before hitting flintmax.

Pascal's Recurrence

The value at row n and column k of Pascal's triangle is the binomial coefficient $C(n, k)$. If we can find a recurrence for Pascal's triangle—a rule for generating the next value in the array based on the previous values—we'll be able to calculate binomial coefficients without any need for factorials.

With arrays, we have lots of flexibility in deciding which previous elements should be used to specify the recurrence. "Previous element" here can mean a value in an earlier row or an earlier value in the same row. I hinted at a recurrence for Pascal's triangle in the initial description: each value is the sum of the two adjacent values immediately above it. Here's how to write that as a recurrence:

$$C(n, k) = C(n - 1, k - 1) + C(n - 1, k)$$

To see why this works, we can interpret each value $C(n, k)$ in Pascal's triangle as the answer to a subset counting problem. Instead of thinking about guests at a pizza party, let's think about counting how many ways there are to pick a set of k of the $(1 + x)$ factors among all of the n factors in $(1 + x)^n$. Every way of picking k factors adds another x^k to the total.

For example, suppose we want to expand $(1 + x)^4$ and see what the coefficient should be for x^3. That would be the binomial coefficient $C(4, 3)$. When we multiply out $(1 + x)(1 + x)(1 + x)(1 + x)$, in each factor of $(1 + x)$ we can pick either the 1 or the x to multiply. To get a term of x^3, we need to pick 1 once and x three times. We could pick the first factor's 1, or the second factor's 1, or the third factor's 1, or the last factor's 1, so there are four ways that we could get x^3. That makes $C(4, 3) = 4$.

Now consider only $n - 1$ repeated $(1 + x)$ factors. The binomial coefficients for $(1 + x)^{n-1}$ are listed in row $n - 1$ of Pascal's triangle. If we want go to from row $n - 1$ to row n, we have to multiply by one extra factor of $(1 + x)$. Again, we need to pick either the 1 or the x for the multiplication. There are two possibilities: either we already have k occurrences of x when we pick factors in $(1 - x)^{k-1}$, in which case we multiply by the 1 of the extra factor, or we have $k - 1$ occurrences of x, in which case we multiply by the x of the extra factor to get k occurrences. That accounting gives the recurrence I just mentioned, which we can use to build the triangle row by row:

$$C(n, k) = C(n - 1, k - 1) + C(n - 1, k)$$

Again, all this means is that to get an entry in Pascal's triangle, we just need to add the two numbers above it.

This recurrence helps us make sense of the value 4 that we calculated for $C(4, 3)$. First, we step back a row in the triangle, from row 4 to row 3, to the coefficients for the expansion of $(1 + x)^3$. We can then either take the x^2 terms in that row that are counted by $C(3, 2)$ and multiply them by x, or take the x^3 terms there that are counted by $C(3, 3)$ and multiply them by 1. Those are the only ways to build an x^3 term in row 4. That means $C(3, 2) + C(3, 3) = C(4, 3)$.

Project 19: Pascal's Triangle, Row by Row

Figure 5-7 shows a Scratch program to calculate up to the nth row of Pascal's triangle using the recurrence we just discussed.

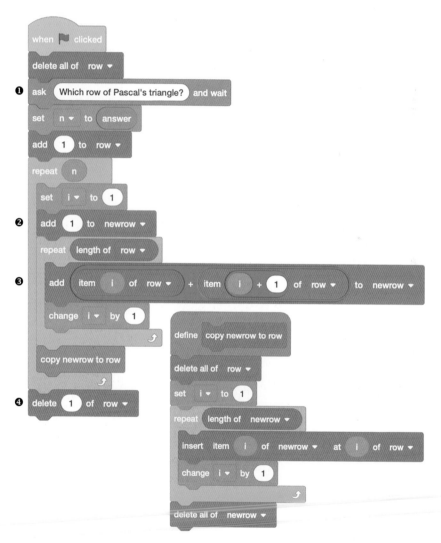

Figure 5-7: Calculating Pascal's triangle, row by row

First, we ask which row to calculate ❶. Then, we loop that many times to work through all the rows up to that one. We use two lists to keep track of the values: row is the previous row in the array, and `newrow` is the current row being calculated. We start each new row with a 1 ❷, then add each adjacent pair of values from `row` to get the next value in `newrow` ❸, as specified by our recurrence. At the end of each cycle through the loop, the custom `copy newrow to row` block copies `newrow` back to `row` to get ready for the next iteration.

The Results

Figure 5-8 shows a sample run of the program, for $n = 8$.

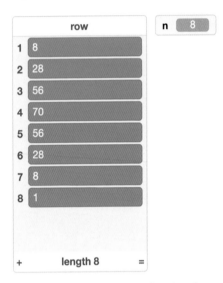

Figure 5-8: Row 8 of Pascal's triangle

Notice that, since Scratch lists are indexed starting with 1 rather than 0, the first element, $C(8, 0) = 1$, isn't listed in the output. It *was* calculated, but we deleted it from the list at the end of the program ❹. This way, Scratch's index numbers match the values of k for the given row. Just imagine that there's an extra 1 at the start of the list, at index 0.

With this approach, we can go much further with calculating exact binomial coefficients. In fact, we don't exceed flintmax until we get to row $n = 56$ of Pascal's triangle. There, the value for $k = 25$ is off (but $k = 26$, 27, and 28 are reported correctly). We also don't have any binomial coefficients reported as Infinity until we get past row 1,000.

Project 20: Drawing Pascal's Triangle

One way to understand Pascal's triangle is to think about how the values of the binomial coefficients are distributed in each row. For example, we can observe that the values are symmetric around the center of the row: 1-2-1, 1-3-3-1, 1-4-6-4-1, and so on.

Mathematically, we can express each row's symmetry by noting that the value at column k in row n is the same as the value at column $n - k$ in the same row. In other words, $C(n, k) = C(n, n - k)$. We can verify this observation by thinking about the subset counting interpretation of Pascal's triangle, discussed earlier in this chapter. To create a subset of k out of n elements, we can say either which k elements should be included or which $n - k$ elements should *not* be included.

Another interesting observation is that the sum of the binomial coefficients in the nth row of Pascal's triangle is 2^n. In row $n = 3$, for example, $1 + 3 + 3 + 1 = 8$, or 2^3, and in row $n = 4$, $1 + 4 + 6 + 4 + 1 = 16$, or 2^4. This also connects with the subset counting interpretation: there are a total of 2^n subsets of a set with n elements because for each of the n elements, there's a choice of two possibilities: to include that element in a subset or not.

One more feature worth noting is that the values in each row are *unimodal*, meaning they start small, increase toward a largest value in the middle, and then get small again. We can make observations like these by looking at the numbers themselves, but features like the values' symmetry and their unimodal structure are even easier to spot if we visualize rows of Pascal's triangle as bar graphs. Also called a *histogram*, a *bar graph* is a chart where the value of each entry is represented by the height of a bar. For example, Figure 5-9 shows a bar graph representing the values in row $n = 10$ of Pascal's triangle. Notice the symmetry of the bar heights.

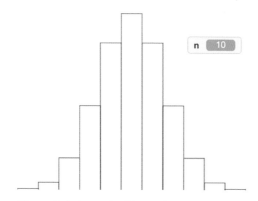

Figure 5-9: Row 10 of Pascal's triangle

To draw bar graphs like these, start with the program in Project 19 (Figure 5-7) for calculating a row of Pascal's triangle. Then, add the custom draw histogram block shown in Figure 5-10. It uses blocks from the Pen extension to draw a bar for each value in the row. Be sure to insert this custom block *before* you delete the 1 at the start of the row (Figure 5-7 ❹), or the symmetry will be spoiled.

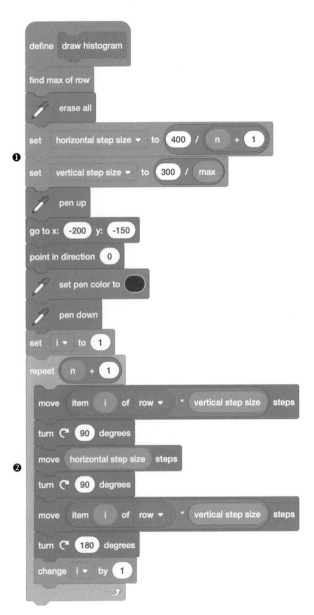

Figure 5-10: Drawing a bar graph from a row

The draw histogram block first takes the row list from the Pascal's triangle program and finds its maximum entry using the custom find max of row block (shown in Figure 5-11). Based on this maximum, we calculate horizontal step size and vertical step size to ensure the drawing will fit on the stage ❶. Then, we use a loop ❷ to draw the bar graph one bar at a time, moving up based on the corresponding value in row, across based on the number of bars to draw, and then back down to start on the next bar.

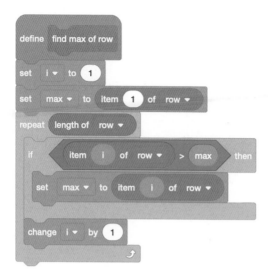

Figure 5-11: Finding the maximum row element

The find max of row block simply cycles through all the values in row, updating the max variable each time it finds a higher value.

The Results

Figure 5-12 shows the bar graphs for two more rows of the triangle.

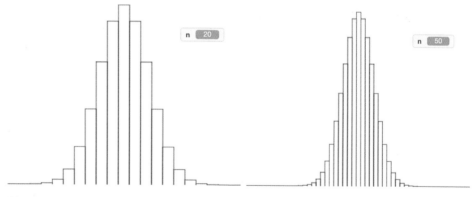

Figure 5-12: Rows 20 (left) and 50 (right) of Pascal's triangle

No matter the row, the shape of the bar graph looks similar. In fact, as *n* increases, the graph gets closer and closer to the famous bell curve of a normal distribution.

Hacking the Code

The new draw histogram block is general enough to draw bar graphs for other datasets besides rows from Pascal's triangle. For example, the code in Figure 5-13 prompts the user to enter a series of numbers—similar to what we did in Project 17 (Figure 4-16), when we were working with difference tables—and then calls the draw histogram block to visualize that data.

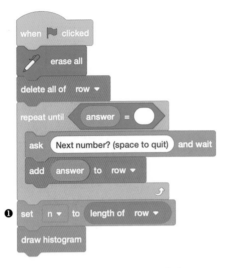

Figure 5-13: Creating a bar graph from a dataset

The draw histogram block expects the data to be in a list called row with a length of n. As long as your program has these features, the bar graph code will work. If all you have is row, you'll need to supply n before drawing the bar graph ❶.

Programming Challenges

5.1 You might notice in a table of values of $n!$ that for larger values of n, the value of $n!$ will end with several zeros. Write a program to predict how many zeros there will be for a given n. In particular, can you predict how many zeros the value of 25! will end with?

5.2 Write a program to extract sequences from Pascal's triangle by stepping down along a diagonal. Use it to consider the diagonal in Pascal's triangle consisting of values of $C(n, 2)$. Identify this sequence in terms of the figurate numbers we discussed in Chapter 4.

5.3 As an integer, the value of a binomial coefficient can be either even or odd. Change the row recurrence program for Pascal's triangle (Project 19) so it shows only 0 or 1, depending on if the binomial coefficient is even or odd. See what kinds of patterns you can find.

Operation Tables Have All the Answers

An *operation table* is a table of values showing the result of a mathematical operation, given different combinations of inputs. For example, you probably learned basic multiplication using a multiplication table, or times table. This type of operation table usually has nine rows and nine columns, and it gives the answer to any multiplication problem where the two numbers being multiplied are indicated by the row and column. If you wanted to multiply 6 times 7, for instance, you would go across the top row (the index row) to find 6 and down the left column (the index column) to find 7. The value where column 6 and row 7 intersect is 42.

We couldn't possibly create a complete multiplication table for all the positive integers because there are infinitely many of them. However, the usual nine-by-nine multiplication table for single-digit numbers has all the information we need to calculate products of longer numbers. Compare this situation with the modular arithmetic we discussed in Chapter 2. Once you pick a modulus, say n, all that matters is the remainder when a number is divided by n. There are only n possible remainders, 0 through $n - 1$. That means any operation table based on modular arithmetic will have a finite number of entries, and an n-by-n table will include them all.

A finite operation table, with its rows and columns, qualifies as an array. In the next project, we'll use Scratch to generate operation tables for a given modulus and then see what kinds of patterns we can find.

Project 21: Infinite Operation Tables with Modular Arithmetic

Our program will prompt the user for a modulus n, then ask them to choose an operation: addition or multiplication. It will then build an n-by-n table showing all possible outcomes of the chosen operation, mod n. For example, say the modulus is 7. The addition table should show the sum of every possible pair of numbers from 0 to 6, interpreted mod 7. The entry at the intersection of column 6 and row 2, for instance, should show (6 + 2) mod 7, which is 1. The multiplication table does the same for multiplication: the intersection of column 6 and row 2 should show (6 · 2) mod 7, which is 5.

We'll build each row of the table as an entry in a Scratch list called table. First, we need some custom blocks to help us get organized. Figure 5-14 shows the setup block, which is called at the start of the program.

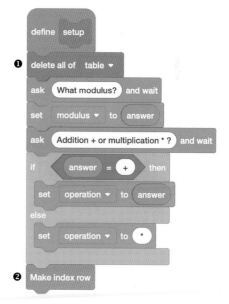

Figure 5-14: Asking what modulus and what operation

In the setup block, we first delete any previous version of table ❶. Then, we prompt the user for the modulus (an integer) and operation (+ or *). Once we have that information, we call the Make index row block ❷, shown in Figure 5-15.

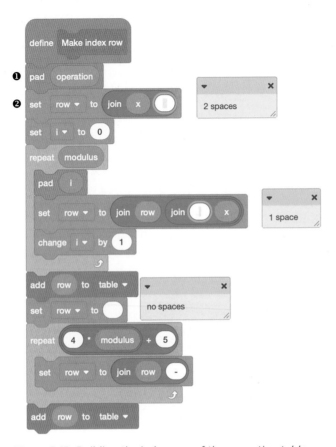

Figure 5-15: Building the index row of the operation table

The Make index row block adds an index row at the top of the table containing labels for the columns, from 0 up to but not including the modulus, along with a + or * symbol to indicate whether it's showing addition or multiplication. We build up the contents of the row as a string in the row variable, using a series of join blocks. We also add an extra row consisting of all dashes, to help set off the column index labels from the contents of the table itself.

Most of the work in this block goes into making the table look pretty, with the columns evenly spaced regardless of whether they contain one-digit or two-digit numbers. To help, we use the custom pad block ❶ (defined in Figure 5-16), which puts either one or two spaces in front of a given string, depending on its length, to ensure that all the numbers in each column will be lined up nicely. If we know how many spaces we need to make the numbers line up, we can put them in directly, as we did in the index row ❷, but otherwise it's better to let the program decide.

NOTE   *The two set x commands inside the pad block might look the same, but they're actually different. The empty space in the first one, which executes when x has a length of 1, has two spaces in it, whereas the bottom one, which executes when x has a length of 2, has only one space.*

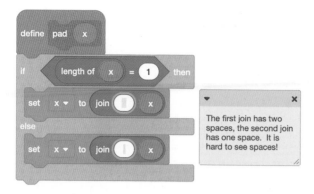

Figure 5-16: Padding a string with one or two spaces

Now that we have all these helper blocks, we can build the operation table, nicely formatted, with the main program code in Figure 5-17.

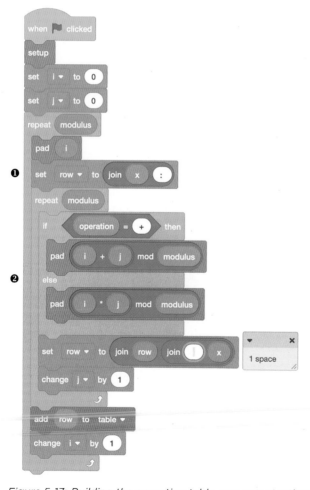

Figure 5-17: Building the operation table, one row at a time

After calling our setup block, we use two nested loops to build the operation table row by row. The outer loop increments the variable i, representing the index number of the current row, while the inner loop increments the variable j, representing the column index number within the row. Each row begins with the row index number itself, followed by a colon ❶. This is necessary because Scratch indexes lists starting from 1, but for our purposes it's more natural to number the rows and columns from 0.

The real work is done in the if...else block inside the inner loop ❷. There, depending on the desired operation, we calculate either i + j or i * j and take the mod of the result, giving us the current entry in the operation table. Once again, we use the pad block to add the appropriate number of spaces before joining the entry to the row being constructed. At the end of each cycle of the outer loop, we have a complete row, which we add to the table list.

The Results

Figure 5-18 shows the resulting addition and multiplication tables for the small modulus $n = 7$.

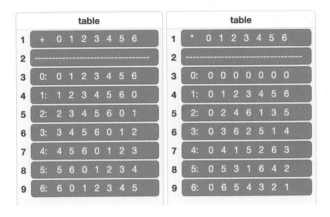

Figure 5-18: Operation tables mod 7

Notice that each table starts with an index row showing the labels of the columns, from 0 to 6. There's also an index column along the left side of the table, showing the labels of the rows (again from 0 to 6).

Using these tables, we can find the sum or product, mod 7, of any two integers. For example, say we want to find (152 + 263) mod 7. First, we need to take mod 7 of each input: 152 mod 7 is 5, and 263 mod 7 is 4. Next, we look in the addition table for the intersection of column 5 and row 4. The value there is 2, so that's our answer. In this way, even though the tables have just seven rows and columns, they can give us the answer for any of the infinite number of positive integers. We just have to take mod 7 of the integers first.

There are several patterns to observe in these mod 7 operation tables:

* For the addition table (on the left in Figure 5-18), the values cycle row by row, shifting one column to the left from one row to the next. The value in the leftmost column of one row wraps back around, becoming the value in the rightmost column of the next row.

- The values in row 0 of the addition table match the values in the table's index row. This indicates that 0 is the *additive identity*: adding 0 to a number doesn't change the number. As far as 0 is concerned, modular addition works just like ordinary addition.

- The *additive inverse* of a number n is the number that needs to be added to n to get 0. In ordinary addition, the additive inverse of a number is that number's negation. For example, the additive inverse of 3 is –3. We don't need to use negative numbers to have additive inverses in modular arithmetic, however. Notice that there's a 0 in every row of the addition table. This means there's a positive number that we can add to get 0, no matter what we start with. That is, every number has an additive inverse for a given modulus. For instance, row 3 has a 0 in the column 4, so 3 + 4 = 0 mod 7.

- For the multiplication table (on the right in Figure 5-18), the values in row 1 match the values in the index row. That means 1 is the *multiplicative identity*: multiplying a number by 1 doesn't change the number. In this sense, modular multiplication is just like regular multiplication.

- There's a 1 in every row and column of the multiplication table except for row and column 0. That means every nonzero number can be multiplied by some other number, called the *multiplicative inverse*, to produce 1 mod 7.

These observations don't just apply to a modulus of 7; they're true of any modulus. Try running the program for some other moduli and you'll see the same patterns.

Hacking the Code

When you start making operation tables for larger moduli, you'll find that the entire contents of each row will no longer fit on the Scratch stage. The complete table is still there behind the scenes, though. If you want to see the whole table at once, you can export the table list to a text file and open it in a text editor or other program, as discussed in Chapter 2. The table will look best if you view it using a *monospaced* font like Courier, where every character has the same width, so the columns all line up. For example, Figure 5-19 shows the exported table for multiplication mod 12.

```
  *    0   1   2   3   4   5   6   7   8   9  10  11
  ----------------------------------------------------
  0:   0   0   0   0   0   0   0   0   0   0   0   0
  1:   0   1   2   3   4   5   6   7   8   9  10  11
  2:   0   2   4   6   8  10   0   2   4   6   8  10
  3:   0   3   6   9   0   3   6   9   0   3   6   9
  4:   0   4   8   0   4   8   0   4   8   0   4   8
  5:   0   5  10   3   8   1   6  11   4   9   2   7
  6:   0   6   0   6   0   6   0   6   0   6   0   6
  7:   0   7   2   9   4  11   6   1   8   3  10   5
  8:   0   8   4   0   8   4   0   8   4   0   8   4
  9:   0   9   6   3   0   9   6   3   0   9   6   3
 10:   0  10   8   6   4   2   0  10   8   6   4   2
 11:   0  11  10   9   8   7   6   5   4   3   2   1
```

Figure 5-19: A multiplication table mod 12

Notice that this table has multiple 0s in some rows and columns. The 0s in row 0 and column 0 are to be expected: multiplication by 0 always yields 0. The other 0s are more interesting. They occur because 12 isn't a prime number. Every factorization of 12 (in fact, every factorization of any multiple of 12) gives two numbers whose product is divisible by 12, and so whose product is 0 mod 12. For instance, in row 4 we have a 0 in columns 0, 3, 6, and 9. Indeed, 4 · 3, 4 · 6, and 4 · 9 are all examples of two numbers that multiply to be 0 mod 12, even though neither number was 0 mod 12 to begin with. These values are known as *zero divisors*, and they don't occur for arithmetic of real numbers. They exist only in modular arithmetic, and only if the modulus isn't prime.

If we cross out all the rows and columns that have extra 0s, as in Figure 5-20, the values that aren't crossed out form a smaller, reduced multiplication table.

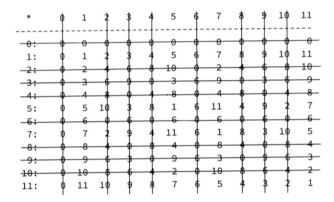

Figure 5-20: A reduced multiplication table mod 12

We're left with a 4×4 table of values, with row and column indices of 1, 5, 7, and 11. Every row and column in this smaller table has a 1 in it, meaning the remaining numbers all have a multiplicative inverse.

Programming Challenges

5.4   If two numbers have no factors in common other than 1, they're said to be *relatively prime*. For example, 6 and 35 are relatively prime, but 35 and 49 are not (they're both divisible by 7). Rewrite the code for the operation tables so that it will produce a reduced multiplication table for a given modulus *n* that includes only rows and columns for numbers that are relatively prime to *n*. For example, for multiplication mod 12, it should produce a table that includes only the four rows and columns that aren't crossed out in Figure 5-20. If the modulus that's supplied is a prime number *p*, it should generate a (*p* – 1)×(*p* – 1) table, omitting row and column 0.

5.5 The *primitive root* of a prime number p is a number whose powers mod p generate all the integers from 1 to $p - 1$. For example, 2 is a primitive root of 11 because:

* 2^{10} = 1,024, and 1,024 mod 11 = 1
* $2^1 = 2$
* 2^8 = 256, and 256 mod 11 = 3
* $2^2 = 4$
* 2^4 = 16, and 16 mod 11 = 5
* 2^9 = 512, and 512 mod 11 = 6
* 2^7 = 128, and 128 mod 11 = 7
* $2^3 = 8$
* 2^6 = 64, and 64 mod 11 = 9
* 2^5 = 32, and 32 mod 11 = 10

On the other hand, 2 isn't a primitive root of 7 because the only powers of 2 mod 7 are 1, 2, and 4. Write a program that asks for a prime number p and returns the first primitive root of p that it finds.

5.6 Spreadsheet programs such as Excel can import text files easily if the files are in CSV format. This format expects there to be a comma between each entry in each row of the input data. Modify the Scratch code for operation tables so that the exported files are formatted in this way.

Conclusion

Arrays are two-dimensional tables of numbers, indexed by row and column. The position of an entry in the table provides two pieces of information—the row and column numbers—that you can sometimes use in a formula to determine the table entry. Scratch doesn't have a built-in array type, but you can represent an array using a list, with each value containing all the array elements for a given row joined together, as we did in building operation tables. Another way to represent an array in Scratch is to build a list for each row of the array, as we did for Pascal's triangle (a list of lists). The right way to represent an array depends on how you want to use it. Scratch is flexible enough to do whatever you want!

Making Codes, and Cracking Them Too

Say you have a secret that you want to share with a friend. You could write it down and pass them a note, but somebody else might see it. Or you could whisper it to them, but somebody might overhear. Think how much better it would be if anyone else who intercepted your message couldn't make sense of it. A secret code!

In this chapter, we'll use Scratch to practice *cryptography*, the art of secret codes. We'll write programs with a few different cryptographic techniques, consider their strengths and weaknesses, and use them to encode messages. Writing a message in code is only half the job, though. There has to be a way to undo the code, or else *nobody* will be able to read it, not even the people you want. We'll look at the other side of the story too, and see how to decode secret messages.

Caesar's Shifty Cipher

Secret codes are important in military applications because commanders need a way to let soldiers in the field know their battle plans, preferably without revealing them to the enemy if they fall into the wrong hands. The Roman general Julius Caesar is credited with devising one of the earliest known methods of encoding messages, for just this purpose. As the story goes, when communicating with his soldiers Caesar used a simple replacement system in which all the letters in the messages (written in Latin, I suppose) were shifted three places to the right. So if there was an A in the message, it was replaced by a D, each B was replaced by an E, and so on. This approach of creating a coded message by shifting the letters in the alphabet is now known as the *Caesar cipher*. The shift doesn't have to be by three; a shift by any number of places will turn a readable message into total gibberish.

Cipher is an old-fashioned word for a procedure or a puzzle. It used to be that doing arithmetic was called *ciphering* because the way numbers get manipulated in big multiplication problems or long division looks like an intricate puzzle. The process of converting a message into a disguised form (*encrypting*) and recovering the original message from its encrypted form (*decrypting*) is also like solving a puzzle, so today *cipher* more commonly refers to a code.

The puzzle for the Caesar cipher can be solved with a two-row table. One row shows the alphabet from A to Z, and the other shows the alphabet shifted over by the appropriate number of places:

A B C D E F G H I J K L M N O P Q R S T U V W X Y Z

D E F G H I J K L M N O P Q R S T U V W X Y Z A B C

It can help to wrap the rows of the table around in a circle to indicate that when we get to the end of the alphabet, we wrap around to the beginning again. Imagine two circles, with an inner alphabet and an outer alphabet, as shown in Figure 6-1.

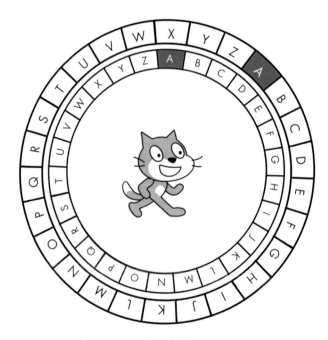

Figure 6-1: Shifting around a circle

If the circles can rotate independently, then they can be used to illustrate the Caesar cipher with different shifts. You can make a tool like this and use it to encrypt and decrypt messages by hand, one letter a time. But why do all that work when Scratch can do it for you?

Project 22: Encryption by a Caesar Shift

In this project, we'll use Scratch to automate the process of encrypting a message with the Caesar cipher. First, we'll put the alphabet into a list, using the custom block shown in Figure 6-2. That way, we can work with the letters by using the numbers that index them in the list.

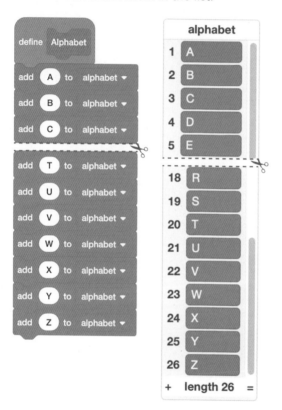

Figure 6-2: Putting the alphabet in a list

The custom Alphabet block builds a list called alphabet, adding letters one at a time. If you want, you can extend the alphabet to include other symbols, like maybe spaces, numbers, and punctuation, but for now we'll keep it to the 26 letters from A to Z.

Next, we'll create a custom block called Initialize to set up the program (see Figure 6-3).

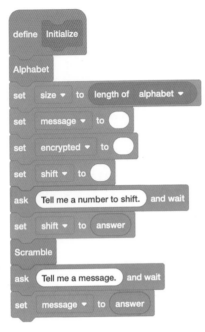

Figure 6-3: The setup code for the
Caesar cipher

In this block, after we call Alphabet, we define size based on the number of characters in the alphabet chosen. Next, we prompt the user for a shift size and a message to encrypt. We then build a scrambled alphabet based on the chosen shift size using the custom Scramble block, shown in Figure 6-4.

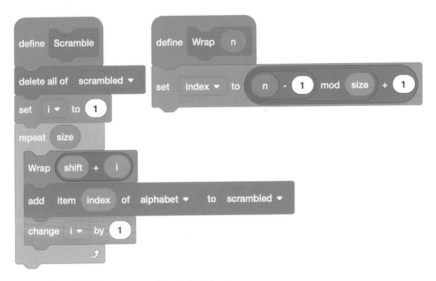

Figure 6-4: Building a scrambled alphabet

The Scramble block builds a list called scrambled by applying the shift to the original alphabet list, one letter at a time. In theory, the letter at index i in the scrambled list should be the same as the letter at index shift + i in the alphabet list. It's not quite that simple, though, since at some point we need to wrap back around to the start of the alphabet. The custom Wrap block, also shown in Figure 6-4, uses mod to recalculate the index when necessary. Because modular arithmetic expects to start from a minimum value of 0 but Scratch wants lists to be indexed starting with 1, we need to subtract 1 before taking the mod, then add 1 again before using the resulting index.

NOTE *The scrambling code is broken out into a separate block to make it easy for us to modify the encryption technique in later programs. All we'll have to do is change how the scrambled encrypting alphabet is constructed.*

Figure 6-5 shows the main program stack.

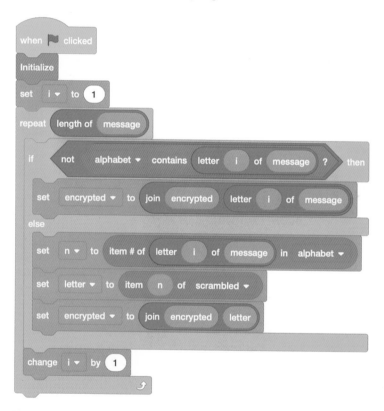

Figure 6-5: The main code for the Caesar cipher

After calling Initialize, we loop through the provided message one character at a time. The if...else block checks if the current message character is included in alphabet. If it is, the program looks up the equivalent shifted character and joins it to the encoded message in the encrypted variable. If the character isn't in the alphabet—for example, if it's a space or punctuation mark—then the program just passes that character through to the encoded message unchanged.

The Results

Figure 6-6 shows the results of two sample runs of the program.

Figure 6-6: Encrypting and decrypting a message

On the left, we've specified a shift of 3 to encode the message "hello!" Scratch keeps track of its characters in uppercase, so when each letter is advanced by 3 we get the encrypted message "KHOOR!" The way we wrote the program, the punctuation doesn't change.

A convenient feature of this program (and of the Caesar cipher itself) is that it can be used to decrypt as well as encrypt. The output on the right shows how we can take the encoded message "KHOOR!" and shift it by 23 to recover our original message of "HELLO!" (now in all caps). Since the alphabet size was 26, an additional shift of 23 after the initial shift of 3 gets us back to 26, which is no shift at all. It would also have worked to enter the second shift as –3 instead of 23 because modulo 26 we get to the same place by going 3 steps backward or 23 steps forward.

Hacking the Code

Because non-alphabet characters aren't encrypted, our code preserves the spaces between words, even as the words themselves are scrambled. This can sometimes be a giveaway, providing clues about the contents of the original message: a one-letter word, for example, is likely *a* or *I*, and *the* and *and* are some of the most common three-letter words. Including a space character in the alphabet will help disguise such clues in the encrypted message by making the original word breaks less obvious. (In addition, some encryption techniques are more effective if the alphabet size is a prime number; this is another reason why adding a space and a couple of other punctuation characters to the alphabet may be a good idea!)

Fortunately, we've written the code in such a way that it works no matter the length of the alphabet, so adding extra characters is easy. The modular arithmetic needed to wrap back around to the start of the alphabet relies on the size variable, which is set based on the length of the Alphabet list at the start of the program. This way, the modulus will be adjusted automatically if the alphabet changes.

Here's another possible improvement: after a few encryptions and decryptions, you may find that you'd like to have a history of the work that Scratch has done. It's easy to add a *log* to hold a record of all of the program's input and output in one place. All you need to do is define a list called log, then add a few blocks (shown in Figure 6-7) to the program to write data to the list. Since the contents of a list can be saved to a file, keeping this log makes it easy to copy the encoded messages into another program, such as a text editor or email client, or back into the input field in the Scratch program for further processing.

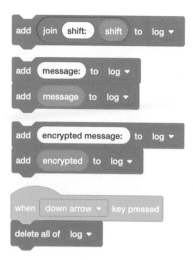

Figure 6-7: Adding a logfile

To create a logfile, add the first two block stacks shown in Figure 6-7, logging the values of shift and message, to the end of the Initialize block (Figure 6-3). Then, add the third stack, logging the encrypted message, to the end of the main program stack (Figure 6-5). The last stack in Figure 6-7 erases the log when you press the down arrow key. You can use this feature to cover your tracks, or to reset the log if it starts to get too long.

Figure 6-8 shows what the log looks like when we decrypt "KHOOR!" by shifting by –3 instead of 23.

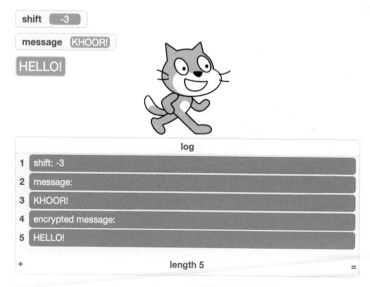

Figure 6-8: Another decryption of "HELLO!"

Because the log list resets only when you press the down arrow key, it will continue to store values over multiple runs of the program, even as the values of shift, message, and encrypted are overwritten.

Caesar's cipher was effective in its time, perhaps because most people couldn't read that well anyway. But in truth, it isn't a very secure method of encryption. If you have a message and you know it's been encrypted by shifting, all you have to do is pass the message through every possible shift factor, and one of them will give you the decrypted text. The number of possible shifts is only the size of the alphabet—in this case, 26. As we'll see in this project, Scratch can work through all the possibilities almost instantaneously.

To create a program for automatically decrypting messages encrypted with a Caesar shift, keep the supporting blocks from the previous project, but modify the main when clicked program stack as shown in Figure 6-9. This updated code will produce a list applying all possible shifts to the encrypted message. When you scroll through the list, the appropriate shift and decoding should jump right out at you.

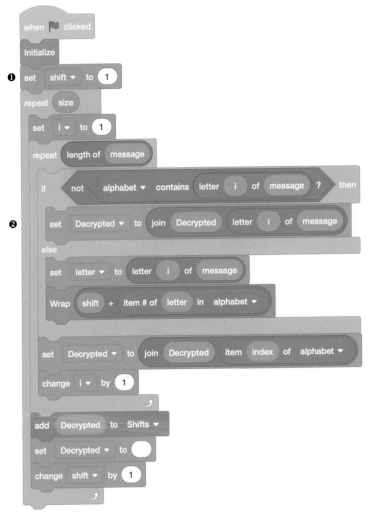

Figure 6-9: Making all possible shifts

We start with an initial shift of 1 ❶ and use a loop to gradually shift through the entire alphabet. Then, we use an inner loop to cycle through the letters of the message and decode them using the current shift factor. At the end of the inner loop, we have a possible decrypted message, which we add to the Shifts list. As in the previous project, we use an if...else block to pass characters through unchanged if they aren't in the alphabet ❷.

We also need to modify the Initialize block from the previous project, as shown in Figure 6-10.

This updated Initialize block manages the Shifts list by deleting its previous contents ❶. We still prompt for a message, but we no longer have to bother with prompting for a shift, since the code generates all possible shifts anyway.

Figure 6-10: Initializing the cracking program

The Results

Suppose you intercept the message "UVA CLYF DLSS OPKKLU, DHZ PA?" Plug it into the decrypting program (you can copy-paste it or enter it by hand) to discover the message in Figure 6-11.

The decrypted message is in line 19 of the Shifts list, which tells us that a shift of 19 was needed to recover the message. So the original message must have been encrypted with a shift of 26 – 19 = 7. With a shift of 7, N becomes U, O becomes V, T becomes A (after wrapping), and so on.

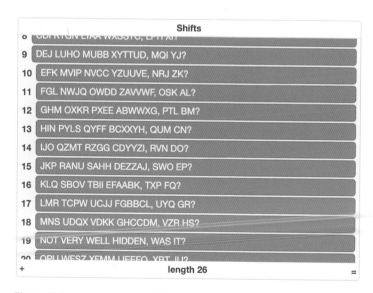

Figure 6-11: Uncovering a shifted message

Programming Challenges

6.1 Use the graphics in Scratch to design a magic decoder ring using a Caesar cipher. The program should animate a ring like the one in Figure 6-1 so that shifted letters line up with the corresponding unshifted letters.

6.2 In the movie *2001: A Space Odyssey*, the sentient computer HAL controlling a spaceship carrying two astronauts on a mission to Jupiter attempts to murder the crew. Apply a Caesar shift of 1 to "HAL" to see if there might be a secret message there about who built him.

6.3 A Caesar shift can translate between different languages, if you're lucky! Apply a shift of 16 to "yes" to translate it into French.

6.4 Find the Caesar shift to decrypt the message "DROBO GSVV LO K RYD DSWO SX DRO YVN DYGX DYXSQRD!"

More Substitution Ciphers

The Caesar cipher is an example of a *substitution cipher*, where each letter of the alphabet is substituted for some other letter of the alphabet. In effect, a substitution cipher scrambles the alphabet, making once-readable words look unfamiliar. With the Caesar cipher, we do the scrambling by shifting all the letters by a set number of positions, but any other scrambling technique would work just as well for encrypting a text. In fact, a nice thing about our original Caesar cipher program is that its main stack (the code in Figure 6-5) can work with any scrambled alphabet, not just one generated through shifting. We can modify the Scramble block (Figure 6-4) to build the scrambled list in some other way, and the program will encode messages accordingly.

If we don't limit ourselves to shifts, how many possibilities for scrambling are there? Well, we have 26 choices for what the letter A becomes, then 25 choices for what B becomes, 24 choices for C, and so on. In all, that gives us 26! (26 factorial) permutations, or over 400 septillion ($4 \cdot 10^{26}$) ways to scramble the alphabet. The Caesar cipher considers only 25 of these permutations (assuming you don't want to use a shift of 0).

The advantage of the Caesar cipher is that it takes only one number, the shift factor, to determine the scrambled alphabet. In other words, if you want to give a friend the key for decoding your shifted messages, all you have to do is whisper that one number to them. Encryption is essentially an addition by the shift factor, and decryption involves undoing the addition. You can undo a shift of *s* by subtracting *s* or by adding 26 – *s*. By contrast, to let your friend in on some other scrambling scheme (perhaps chosen randomly from the 26! possible permutations), you'd need to provide 25 separate pieces of information before they'd know how to decode your messages. You'd have to say what each letter from A to Y becomes, after which Z has to go in the only slot left. That's a lot of extra information to keep track of!

Encryption by Modular Multiplication

Here's a different idea. The Caesar cipher scrambles the alphabet by shifting, which can be thought of as addition modulo 26. What if we scramble the alphabet by *multiplication* modulo 26 rather than addition? That is, we can take each letter's position in the alphabet and multiply it by some number modulo 26 to get the position of the letter it should be replaced with. To get us started, Figure 6-12 shows an operation table for mod 26 multiplication. (You can generate this table yourself using the code from Project 21 in Chapter 5.)

*	0	1	2	3	4	5	6	7	8	9	10	11	12	13	14	15	16	17	18	19	20	21	22	23	24	25
0:	0	0	0	0	0	0	0	0	0	0	0	0	0	0	0	0	0	0	0	0	0	0	0	0	0	0
1:	0	1	2	3	4	5	6	7	8	9	10	11	12	13	14	15	16	17	18	19	20	21	22	23	24	25
2:	0	2	4	6	8	10	12	14	16	18	20	22	24	0	2	4	6	8	10	12	14	16	18	20	22	24
3:	0	3	6	9	12	15	18	21	24	1	4	7	10	13	16	19	22	25	2	5	8	11	14	17	20	23
4:	0	4	8	12	16	20	24	2	6	10	14	18	22	0	4	8	12	16	20	24	2	6	10	14	18	22
5:	0	5	10	15	20	25	4	9	14	19	24	3	8	13	18	23	2	7	12	17	22	1	6	11	16	21
6:	0	6	12	18	24	4	10	16	22	2	8	14	20	0	6	12	18	24	4	10	16	22	2	8	14	20
7:	0	7	14	21	2	9	16	23	4	11	18	25	6	13	20	1	8	15	22	3	10	17	24	5	12	19
8:	0	8	16	24	6	14	22	4	12	20	2	10	18	0	8	16	24	6	14	22	4	12	20	2	10	18
9:	0	9	18	1	10	19	2	11	20	3	12	21	4	13	22	5	14	23	6	15	24	7	16	25	8	17
10:	0	10	20	4	14	24	8	18	2	12	22	6	16	0	10	20	4	14	24	8	18	2	12	22	6	16
11:	0	11	22	7	18	3	14	25	10	21	6	17	2	13	24	9	20	5	16	1	12	23	8	19	4	15
12:	0	12	24	10	22	8	20	6	18	4	16	2	14	0	12	24	10	22	8	20	6	18	4	16	2	14
13:	0	13	0	13	0	13	0	13	0	13	0	13	0	13	0	13	0	13	0	13	0	13	0	13	0	13
14:	0	14	2	16	4	18	6	20	8	22	10	24	12	0	14	2	16	4	18	6	20	8	22	10	24	12
15:	0	15	4	19	8	23	12	1	16	5	20	9	24	13	2	17	6	21	10	25	14	3	18	7	22	11
16:	0	16	6	22	12	2	18	8	24	14	4	20	10	0	16	6	22	12	2	18	8	24	14	4	20	10
17:	0	17	8	25	16	7	24	15	6	23	14	5	22	13	4	21	12	3	20	11	2	19	10	1	18	9
18:	0	18	10	2	20	12	4	22	14	6	24	16	8	0	18	10	2	20	12	4	22	14	6	24	16	8
19:	0	19	12	5	24	17	10	3	22	15	8	1	20	13	6	25	18	11	4	23	16	9	2	21	14	7
20:	0	20	14	8	2	22	16	10	4	24	18	12	6	0	20	14	8	2	22	16	10	4	24	18	12	6
21:	0	21	16	11	6	1	22	17	12	7	2	23	18	13	8	3	24	19	14	9	4	25	20	15	10	5
22:	0	22	18	14	10	6	2	24	20	16	12	8	4	0	22	18	14	10	6	2	24	20	16	12	8	4
23:	0	23	20	17	14	11	8	5	2	25	22	19	16	13	10	7	4	1	24	21	18	15	12	9	6	3
24:	0	24	22	20	18	16	14	12	10	8	6	4	2	0	24	22	20	18	16	14	12	10	8	6	4	2
25:	0	25	24	23	22	21	20	19	18	17	16	15	14	13	12	11	10	9	8	7	6	5	4	3	2	1

Figure 6-12: Multiplication mod 26

This table gives all possible products of two numbers modulo 26. For example, to multiply 9 by 5, look at row 9 and column 5. The entry where they intersect is 19, so 9 · 5 is 19 mod 26. That makes sense, since we know that 9 · 5 is "really" 45, and 45 leaves a remainder of 19 when it's divided by 26.

For a row (or column) of this table to lead to a successful scrambling of the alphabet, it needs to include every number from 0 to 25—that is, it must be a permutation (or reordering) of the table's index. Not every row works. For example, row 4 begins (0, 4, 8, . . .) and starts repeating itself at column 13. Meanwhile, the values in row 13 simply alternate back and forth between 0 and 13, which would turn all the letters in a message into either As or Ns. Not very useful!

The usable rows (and columns) are the ones indexed by numbers that are relatively prime to 26, meaning they share no common factors with 26 other than 1. There are 12 of them: rows 1, 3, 5, 7, 9, 11, 15, 17, 19, 21, 23, and 25. These rows all contain permutations of the numbers between 0 and 25. For example, multiplying the letters of the alphabet by 3 mod 26 would give the following cipher:

A B C D E F G H I J K L M N O P Q R S T U V W X Y Z

C F I L O R U X A D G J M P S V Y B E H K N Q T W Z

You could build the scrambled row by counting ahead by three letters each time (A B **C**, D E **F**, G H **I**,...), wrapping around at Z to begin again, until the entire alphabet has been assigned.

To implement a multiplication-based cipher using our code from Project 22, all we have to do is make one small change to our Scramble block from earlier, as illustrated in Figure 6-13.

Figure 6-13: Multiply, don't add!

By changing + to *, we tell the program to encrypt messages using modular multiplication rather than modular addition.

Decryption by Modular Multiplication

Now let's consider decrypting. We decrypted a Caesar shift by undoing the addition. To undo a shift of 3 letters to the right, for example, we shifted 3 letters to the left (or 26 − 3 = 23 more to the right, since the arithmetic is mod 26). To undo a multiplication by 3, we need to divide by 3, but there's no room for fractions or decimal places in modular arithmetic. If the original modular multiplication by 3 gave a result of 14, we can't turn around and divide by 3 to say we want letter 4.66 of the alphabet.

Fortunately, there's still a way to undo the multiplication. We have to find the modular inverse of the multiplier and use that as the decryption key. The *modular inverse* is the multiplicative inverse, where the multiplication is interpreted using modular arithmetic. Given a modulus m—in this case, 26—multiplying a number by its modular inverse yields 1 mod m. For example, notice in the multiplication table in Figure 6-12 that there's a 1 in row 3, located at column 9. This tells us that 9 is the modular inverse of 3 mod 26. To prove it, check the math: $3 \cdot 9 = 27$, and 27 mod 26 = 1.

If you're used to arithmetic giving a multiplicative inverse as a fraction, it may seem strange to see a multiplicative inverse that's an integer, let alone an integer that's greater than the original number. Shouldn't the multiplicative inverse be something small? After all, in ordinary arithmetic the multiplicative inverse of 3 is 1/3, since $3 \cdot 1/3$ is 1. All that matters for an inverse, though, is that the product is 1. With ordinary arithmetic, you get 1 by multiplying n by $1/n$. With modular arithmetic, you get 1 by multiplying n by some other integer.

Since 9 is the multiplicative inverse of 3 mod 26, we can use a multiplier of 9 to decrypt a message that was encrypted with a multiplier of 3. The log shown in Figure 6-14 confirms this.

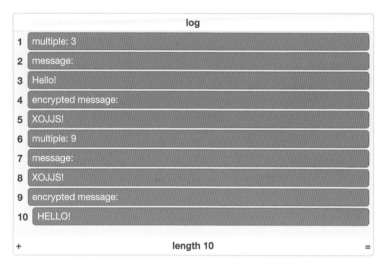

Figure 6-14: Uncovering a multiplied message

First, we use a multiplier of 3 to encrypt the message "Hello!" Then, we use 9, the modular inverse of 3 mod 26, to "encrypt" the result, which restores the original message.

Project 24: The Modular Inverse Is the Key

We've established that to recover a message encrypted through modular multiplication, we need the modular inverse. In this project, we'll look at how to find a modular inverse to aid in the decryption process.

One way to find a modular inverse is to just look for it: study the operation table for multiplication mod alphabet size and see what multiple of m gives the answer 1. That multiple is the modular inverse. That's the approach we took in the last section, examining the mod 26 multiplication table in Figure 6-12 to determine that the modular inverse of 3 is 9. Now let's automate that process with Scratch so we can easily find the modular inverse for any number and any modulus. Figure 6-15 shows how.

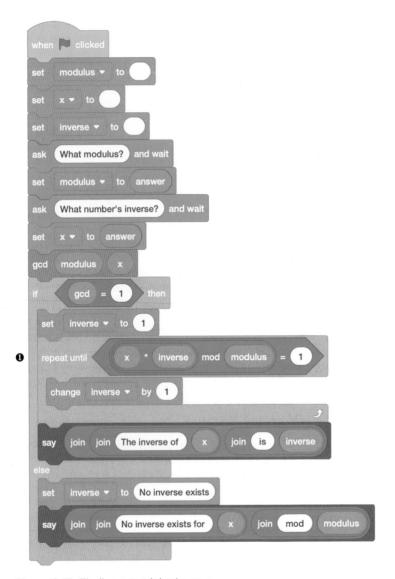

Figure 6-15: Finding a modular inverse

The program first prompts for a modulus and a number to invert. These two values must be relatively prime in order for the number to have a modular inverse. We test for this using the custom gcd block we built for Project 9 back in Chapter 2 (see Figure 2-17 on page 38). If the GCD is 1, the values are relatively prime, so we use a loop to test every possible inverse, starting from 1, until we find the one where x * inverse mod modulus = 1 **❶**. This is the programmatic equivalent of scanning a row of the operation table until we find the column with a 1 in it.

The Results

Figure 6-16 shows some output demonstrating how the code works.

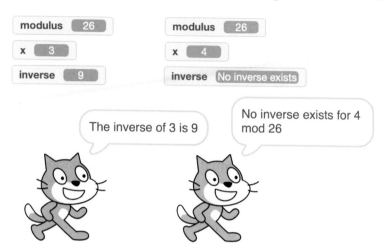

Figure 6-16: Modular inverse calculations

The program confirms that 9 is the inverse of 3 mod 26. It also correctly concludes that 4 mod 26 has no modular inverse, since 4 and 26 aren't relatively prime.

Hacking the Code

The trial-and-error approach in our modular inverse program isn't bad for a small alphabet (and, by extension, a small modulus), but it would be better to have a more focused algorithm to quickly calculate the modular inverse of any number for any modulus. As with the gcd block, we can reuse part of a program we wrote earlier for this: the calculation of the greatest common divisor via Euclid's algorithm from Project 9 in Chapter 2.

Remember that Euclid's algorithm worked to calculate the GCD d of two given numbers b and a with a sequence of divisions, ending with the GCD as the last nonzero remainder. To use this algorithm to find a modular inverse, set b to the modulus and a to the number whose inverse you want to find. Work through the algorithm as usual, keeping track of the arithmetic of the divisions. Then, step through it backward, looking for an equation that puts 1 on one side and both a and b on the other.

For example, if we wanted to find the modular inverse of 3 mod 26, we could first pass those numbers through Euclid's algorithm:

$$26 = 8 \cdot 3 + 2$$
$$3 = 1 \cdot 2 + 1$$
$$2 = 2 \cdot 1 + 0$$

The last nonzero remainder, 1, is the GCD. Next, we need to unwind the steps to find a combination of 26 and 3 that equals 1. Rewriting the middle equation in the algorithm, we get $1 = 3 - 2$. Rewriting the top equation in the algorithm, we get $2 = 26 - 8 \cdot 3$. Then, substituting $26 - 8 \cdot 3$ for the 2 in the middle equation, we get

1 = 3 – (26 – 8 · 3). Overall, the right side of this equation has one 3 and then eight more 3s in the parentheses, so 1 + 8 = 9 of them in all, along with –1 · 26. We can combine the pieces to see 1 = 9 · 3 – 26. This tells us that 1 = 9 · 3 mod 26, so 9 is the modular inverse of 3. There's a programming challenge coming up to make this approach work in general.

More Encryption Options with Linear Transformations

You might think we haven't gained much by switching from modular addition to modular multiplication. After all, for an alphabet of size 26 there were 26 possible shifted alphabets, and there are only 12 possible multiplied alphabets. However, we can get a much bigger set of scrambled alphabets by combining both approaches: multiply *and* shift. That is, we can apply any of the 26 possible shifts to each of the 12 scrambled alphabets obtained through multiplication, giving us 26 · 12 = 312 potential alphabets. That's many more possibilities to hide a message.

The general rule for this combined approach is that we scramble the alphabet by replacing the letter whose index is i with the letter whose index is $m \cdot i + s$. In other words, we multiply the index by m, then add a constant s. If we picked values for m and s and graphed the results of this formula for every value of i, we'd find that the graph shows a straight line with a slope of m. For example, say we set m to 2 and s to 3. If we graph the function $2i + 3$, the line passes through the points (0, 3), (1, 5), (2, 7), (3, 9), (4, 11), (5, 13), and (6, 15), as shown in Figure 6-17.

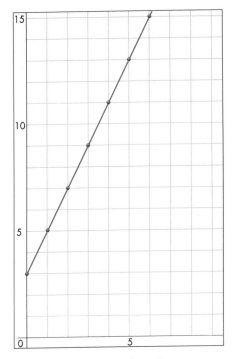

Figure 6-17: A graph of 2i + 3

Because they produce straight lines, "multiply plus a constant" formulas like $m \cdot i + s$ are known as *linear functions*. By extension, a "multiply and shift" encryption process is called a *linear transformation*. As long as the multiplier m is chosen to be relatively prime to the alphabet size, the encryption will work.

Project 25: Encryption by a Linear Transformation

Let's adapt our Caesar cipher code from Project 22 to handle linear transformations. First, we'll update the Initialize block as shown in Figure 6-18.

Figure 6-18: Linear transformation encryption

We now prompt for both a shift and a multiplier, instead of just a shift like before. Notice also the extra code to maintain the log list. Next, we'll modify the Scramble block to match Figure 6-19.

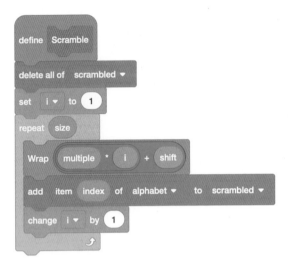

Figure 6-19: Wrapping with a linear transformation

This updated Scramble block still uses the original Wrap block from Figure 6-4. The input to Wrap implements the $m \cdot i + s$ linear function to scramble the alphabet.

The Results

Figure 6-20 shows an example of the linear transformation program in action. It encrypts the message "TOP SECRET!" using a multiplier of 3 and a shift of 5.

Figure 6-20: Encrypting with a linear transformation

To decrypt the resulting message, we need to undo both the shift and the multiplication. Undoing the shift is easy: for an original shift of s, we instead perform a shift of $-s$. And as we've discussed, to undo a multiplication by m, we can multiply by the modular inverse of m. We'll perform these operations separately, by running the encrypted message through the linear transformation program twice: once for the shift and once for the multiplication.

First, we undo the shift of 5 with a shift of -5, as shown in Figure 6-21. We use a multiplier of 1, meaning we're effectively doing no multiplication at all.

Figure 6-21: Undoing the shift

Next, we need to take the result and feed it back into the linear transformation program to undo the multiplication. We know that the modular inverse of 3 mod 26 is 9, so that's the multiplier we use in Figure 6-22. This time, we use a shift of 0 to focus just on reversing the multiplication. The result is the original message.

TOP SECRET!

Figure 6-22: Undoing the multiplication

In all, only two numbers determine an encryption by linear transformation: the shift and the multiplier. Likewise, only two numbers are needed to decrypt the message. It's a pretty compact secret key!

Programming Challenges

6.5 You've seen how to decrypt a linear transformation cipher in two separate steps, first undoing the shift and then undoing the multiplication. Is it possible to combine these into a single step? For example, could you decrypt the message MXA JTNGTM!" from Figure 6-20 by running the linear transformation program once, with a shift of –5 and a multiplier of 9? As it turns out, this won't work, but there's a different shift factor that will. Think about what it could be, and why.

6.6 Use what you've learned from Challenge 6.5 to write a Scratch program that takes in a multiplier and shift for a linear transformation encryption and calculates the modular inverse and appropriate shift to perform the decryption in one step.

6.7 What goes wrong in a linear transformation encryption if the multiplier isn't relatively prime to the alphabet size?

6.8 Modify the Project 23 code for cracking a Caesar shift (Figure 6-9) so the program lists all possible decryptions for all 312 possible linear transformation ciphers.

6.9 Any permutation or scrambling of the alphabet can be the key for a substitution cipher. Write a Scratch program that will generate a random scrambling of the alphabet. The pick random operator block might come in handy for this.

(continued)

> **6.10** Write a program to calculate modular inverses using Euclid's algorithm, as discussed in "Hacking the Code" on page 115. You'll probably want to keep track of quotients and remainders as lists and work your way backward up the lists to unwind the steps.

Unbreakable One-Time Pad Ciphers

A *one-time pad cipher* is a technique that uses one text (the key) to encrypt or decrypt another text (the message). The encryption takes the first character of the message and shifts it by the position of the first character in the key. It then shifts the second character by the position of the second character in the key, and so on. Every character in the message uses its own encryption scheme, with the alphabet essentially being rescrambled for each letter.

To illustrate, let's say we want to encrypt the message "Hello" using the word "Scratch" as a key. (The key should always be at least as long as, if not longer than, the message.) The first letter of the key, S, is the 19th letter of the alphabet, so we should shift the first letter in the message, H, by 19 positions, yielding the letter A (after wrapping around at Z). The second letter of the key, C, is the third letter of the alphabet, so we should shift the second letter of the message, E, by 3 positions, yielding the letter H. If we keep going like this, we'll end up with "AHDMI" as the coded message. Using the key to do the shifts in reverse decrypts the message.

Typically, one-time pads are used to share longer coded messages, using correspondingly longer keys. The key might be a literal notepad, with a long handwritten sequence of random letters determining the shifts to be used. Or it could be any other text that the sender and recipient of the message agree to share, such as the lyrics of a song, a passage in a book, or an article posted on the internet. The important thing is to keep the key a secret.

One-time pads are much stronger codes than the simpler ciphers we discussed earlier in the chapter. In fact, if you use a truly random sequence of characters for the key and you never use the same key twice (hence *one-time* pad), your coded messages will be impossible to crack. The same cannot be said about any secret code based on a fixed permutation of the alphabet, whether it's a Caesar cipher, a linear transformation, or any other scrambling algorithm. This is because, as mentioned earlier, the English language has patterns and regularities in it that provide clues about the message.

Even if we remove the spaces between words to conceal obvious giveaways like one-letter words (almost certain *I* or *a*) and recurring three-letter words (quite possibly *the* or *and*), there are other patterns that can shine through in a scrambled alphabet. For example, only certain letters commonly appear twice in a row in English: there are plenty of words with double Es, Ss, and Ts, far fewer with double As or double Zs, and virtually none with double Qs or double Js. Two-letter sequences like TH and CK are also common.

More broadly, letters like E and A occur much more often in a given English text than letters like Q and Z, so counting the *frequency*, meaning the number of occurrences, of each letter in an encrypted message—especially a long message—can give a good clue about the encryption scheme. To prove it, we'll write a program to calculate letter frequencies and test it on a text encrypted with a Caesar shift. Then we'll write a program to implement a one-time pad cipher and test its result as well. We should see that the one-time pad cipher eliminates any regular patterns.

Project 26: Frequency Analysis for Cracking Codes

The goal for this project is to create a program that counts how many times each letter is used in an encrypted message, potentially providing clues about the encryption scheme based on how many times different letters are used in a typical unencrypted English text. We'll need to take advantage of Scratch's text processing capabilities for this. In particular, we'll use the green length of and letter of blocks together in a loop to examine a text one character at a time. Figure 6-23 shows the program.

Figure 6-23: Counting how many times each letter is used

We use two separate lists: alphabet, which is built up at the start of the program with the same Alphabet block first defined in Figure 6-2, and frequency, where we store the number of occurrences of each letter of the alphabet. To begin, we fill frequency with 26 0s. Then we take in a text to process from the user and loop through it one character at a time. The item # of letter i of text in alphabet does a reverse lookup of the *i*th character of the text in alphabet. For example, if the character is C, this will give us 3, C's position in the alphabet list. We add 1 to the entry at the same position in the frequency list to count that character ❶.

Hacking the Code

The code in Figure 6-24 is a nice little addition to the program that adds labels to the frequency list. Place it at the end, after the repeat loop.

Figure 6-24: Adding a label to each entry in the frequency list

After all the counting is done, this extra code labels each entry in the frequency list with the letter of the alphabet it represents. This way, you won't have to remind yourself that letter A is 1, letter B is 2, and so on.

The Results

Let's put the frequency analysis program to work. We'll start with a reasonably sized unencrypted text, the first chapter of *Alice's Adventures in Wonderland*, to get a feel for the normal frequencies of letters in ordinary English. You don't have to type the whole text out yourself; just look it up online and copy-paste it when Scratch Cat asks for your input. Figure 6-25 shows the results.

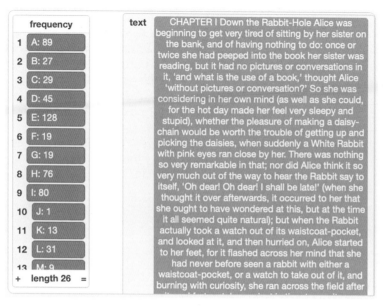

frequency		text	CHAPTER I Down the Rabbit-Hole Alice was beginning to get very tired of sitting by her sister on the bank, and of having nothing to do: once or twice she had peeped into the book her sister was reading, but it had no pictures or conversations in it, 'and what is the use of a book,' thought Alice 'without pictures or conversation?' So she was considering in her own mind (as well as she could, for the hot day made her feel very sleepy and stupid), whether the pleasure of making a daisy-chain would be worth the trouble of getting up and picking the daisies, when suddenly a White Rabbit with pink eyes ran close by her. There was nothing so very remarkable in that; nor did Alice think it so very much out of the way to hear the Rabbit say to itself, 'Oh dear! Oh dear! I shall be late!' (when she thought it over afterwards, it occurred to her that she ought to have wondered at this, but at the time it all seemed quite natural); but when the Rabbit actually took a watch out of its waistcoat-pocket, and looked at it, and then hurried on, Alice started to her feet, for it flashed across her mind that she had never before seen a rabbit with either a waistcoat-pocket, or a watch to take out of it, and burning with curiosity, she ran across the field after
1	A: 89		
2	B: 27		
3	C: 29		
4	D: 45		
5	E: 128		
6	F: 19		
7	G: 19		
8	H: 76		
9	I: 80		
10	J: 1		
11	K: 13		
12	L: 31		
13	M: 9		
+	length 26 =		

Figure 6-25: Analyzing character frequencies in an unencrypted text (down the rabbit hole...)

As you can see, the text contains lots of Es and As, but only one J. If you scroll to the bottom of the list, you'll find there's one Q and no Xs or Zs. This is a pretty typical distribution of letters for an English-language text.

Now try using our original Caesar cipher program from Project 22 to encrypt the same *Alice's Adventures in Wonderland* chapter, shifting the alphabet by three places. Plug the encrypted text into the frequency analysis program. Figure 6-26 shows the result.

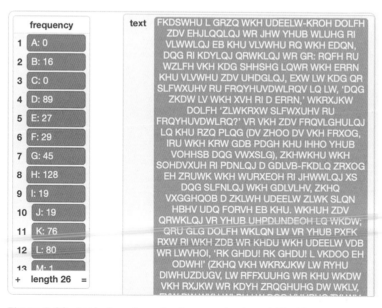

frequency		text	FKDSWHU L GRZQ WKH UDEELW-KROH DOLFH ZDV EHJLQQLQJ WR JHW YHUB WLUHG RI VLWWLQJ EB KHU VLVWHU RQ WKH EDQN, DQG RI KDYLQJ QRWKLQJ WR GR: RQFH RU WZLFH VKH KDG SHHSHG LQWR WKH ERRN KHU VLVWHU ZDV UHDGLQJ, EXW LW KDG QR SLFWXUHV RU FRQYHUVDWLRQV LQ LW, 'DQG ZKDW LV WKH XVH RI D ERRN,' WKRXJKW DOLFH 'ZLWKRXW SLFWXUHV RU FRQYHUVDWLRQ?' VR VKH ZDV FRQVLGHULQJ LQ KHU RZQ PLQG (DV ZHOO DV VKH FRXOG, IRU WKH KRW GDB PDGH KHU IHHO YHUB VOHHSB DQG VWXSLG), ZKHWKHU WKH SOHDVXUH RI PDNLQJ D GDLVB-FKDLQ ZRXOG EH ZRUWK WKH WURXEOH RI JHWWLQJ XS DQG SLFNLQJ WKH GDLVLHV, ZKHQ VXGGHQOB D ZKLWH UDEELW ZLWK SLQN HBHV UDQ FORVH EB KHU. WKHUH ZDV QRWKLQJ VR YHUB UHPDUNDEOH LQ WKDW; QRU GLG DOLFH WKLQN LW VR YHUB PXFK RXW RI WKH ZDB WR KHDU WKH UDEELW VDB WR LWVHOI, 'RK GHDU! RK GHDU! L VKDOO EH ODWH!' (ZKHQ VKH WKRXJKW LW RYHU DIWHUZDUGV, LW RFFXUUHG WR KHU WKDW VKH RXJKW WR KDYH ZRQGHUHG DW WKLV,
1	A: 0		
2	B: 16		
3	C: 0		
4	D: 89		
5	E: 27		
6	F: 29		
7	G: 45		
8	H: 128		
9	I: 19		
10	J: 19		
11	K: 76		
12	L: 80		
13	M: 1		
+	length 26 =		

Figure 6-26: Analyzing character frequencies in a shifted text

I can't read the encrypted message, but I do notice that the word *DQG* appears lots of times, which is a clue. More importantly, there's still a strong pattern in the frequencies of letters that suggests how the most common letters have been encoded. Of course, the pattern matches the original message perfectly, shifted three places: you can see the original frequency for A showing up at D, the original frequency for E showing up at H, and so on. The zeros at A and C are from X and Z wrapped around. Looking at this output, even if I didn't know what the original text was, I could make a good guess as to which letter is E.

In theory, a one-time pad cipher should eliminate these patterns, causing every letter in the encrypted text to appear with roughly the same frequency. We'll find out in the next project.

Project 27: Encryption with a One-Time Pad

We can program a one-time pad encryption in Scratch by making just a few changes to the encryption programs we've written so far. Figure 6-27 shows the Initialize block.

Figure 6-27: Setup code for the one-time pad

This block asks for the encoding key and the message. It also asks if the user wants to encrypt or decrypt ❶, so we can use the same program for both operations. Depending on the answer, the variable `action` is assigned a value of 1 or -1. This value is incorporated into the arithmetic of the shift, such that encryption involves adding the shift and decryption involves subtracting it.

Notice that the `Initialize` block sets up a log so we can scroll through a history of the program's use. It also calls a custom `Trim` key block, which is defined in Figure 6-28.

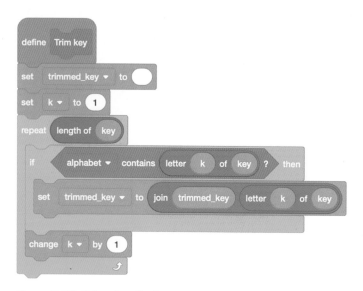

Figure 6-28: Trimming the key

In the `Trim` key block, we take the text that will be used to encrypt the message and remove any characters (like spaces or punctuation) that aren't in the alphabet. The variable `trimmed_key` starts out empty. Then, the `repeat` loop steps through the key character by character; it ignores characters that aren't in the `alphabet` list and puts the rest of the characters into `trimmed_key`.

Figure 6-29 shows the main program code.

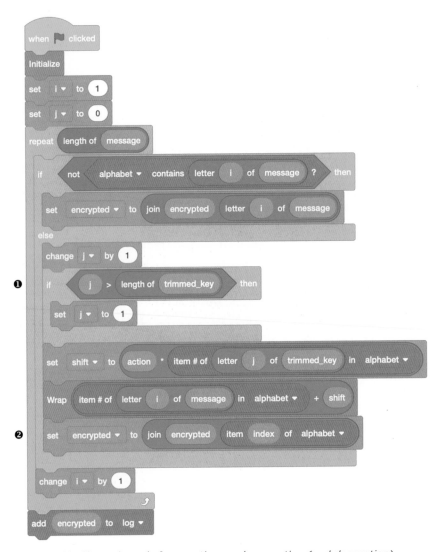

Figure 6-29: The main code for one-time pad encryption (and decryption)

In this stack, we move character by character through the message (using index i) and the trimmed key (using index j), determining the shift for the current character in the message based on the current character in the key. We use an if statement ❶ to wrap back around to the start of the trimmed key if there are more characters in the message than in the key. As I mentioned earlier in the chapter, though, it's best to use a key that's at least as long as the message. A shorter key is a vulnerability: if the key starts to repeat, frequency analysis can reveal information about the key length and encoding phrase. A one-character key, for example, is equivalent to a Caesar shift!

The real work is done in the set block ❷. It builds the encrypted message one character at a time by shifting the original character by an amount determined by the corresponding character in the key. We use the original Wrap block from Figure 6-4 to get the index for the appropriate letter. Notice also that we multiply by action (either 1 or -1) when setting the value of shift. As mentioned previously, this allows the program to work for encryption and decryption by shifting either forward or backward.

The Results

To see how secure one-time pad encryption is compared to simple alphabet scramblings like the Caesar cipher, let's use our program to encrypt the same *Alice's Adventures in Wonderland* chapter as before. For that, we need to choose a key. I'll use the nonsense poem "Jabberwocky," shown in Figure 6-30, to keep in the Lewis Carroll spirit.

Figure 6-30: The one-time pad key

Encode the *Alice* chapter using the one-time pad program in encryption mode, find the encrypted text in the log, and copy-paste it into the frequency analysis program from the previous project. The result should look something like Figure 6-31.

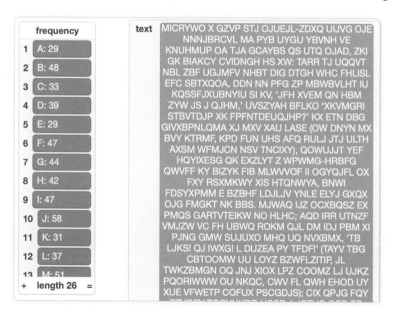

Figure 6-31: Analyzing character frequencies in text encrypted with a one-time pad

As you can see, the distribution of letters is now much flatter: no one letter stands out as being used much more (or less) frequently than the others, so frequency analysis doesn't provide any clues for cracking the code. What's more, the one-time pad has also eliminated regular patterns from the encrypted text itself. Whereas the Caesar-shifted version (Figure 6-26) showed *DQG* at every instance of the word *and*, now each occurrence of *and* is encoded differently: first *ZKI*, then

JFH, and so on. Without the key, decrypting the text seems like an impossible task; there are no clues to help you. And just imagine if spaces and punctuation were included in the alphabet and scrambled along with the letters—the encoded message would look like letter soup!

Programming Challenges

6.11 A *cryptogram* is a word puzzle based on a scrambled alphabet, not necessarily a Caesar shift or a linear transformation. Write a Scratch program to help solve cryptograms by keeping track of letters as they're guessed and showing progress with a partial decryption. Here's an example of a cryptogram for you to solve. As a clue to help you get started, this cryptogram uses M to stand for S. You can look at patterns and letter frequencies to guess the other letters.

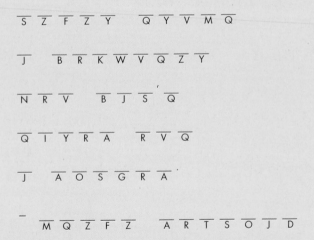

6.12 Write a Scratch program to remove spaces and punctuation from a text string so all that's left is a string of letters and numbers. This could be useful to remove word-break clues from an encrypted message.

Conclusion

Scratch isn't just for processing numbers; it's just as good at processing text. Any transformation rule that's reversible can be the basis of an encryption algorithm for sharing secrets, but some rules (like using a one-time pad) are better than others (like basic shifts) for keeping secrets safe. You can always use techniques like frequency analysis to look for clues about how to decode a message.

Experiments in Counting

Combinatorics is a branch of mathematics that's often called *the art of counting*. The "art" is in coming up with a way to organize a counting problem so that the objects being counted can be generated elegantly.

Combinatorics has many important applications. In computer science, for example, combinatorial algorithms are good for tasks such as sorting and searching through data. In telecommunications, combinatorics provides error-correcting codes and network protocols for efficient data transmission. In genetics, it's used to analyze and model genes to understand heredity and genetic variation.

This chapter explores two classic examples from the world of combinatorics: Catalan numbers and partitions. For each example, we'll develop a strategy for listing every instance of a pattern that satisfies a certain set of rules. Then, we'll look for a recurrence formula to count all the instances without having to actually list them all.

What Are Counting Problems?

In some counting problems, there's a parameter indicating a measure of size or quantity: say, the counting number *n*. We want to know how many ways there are to use *n* to generate distinct objects. A classic example is figuring out how many ways there are to arrange *n* items. Each unique ordering of items is considered to be a different object. (The answer is *n* factorial, as we saw in Chapter 5.)

In other counting problems, there's a single object determined by the parameter *n*, and we want to measure some aspect of that object. For example, we considered square numbers when we discussed sequences in Chapter 4. There, the object associated with *n* was a square of side length *n*, which can be built with n^2 1×1 subsquares. The sequence of squares is determined by considering how many points there are for *n* = 1, 2, 3, and so on.

I like to think of the parameter in a counting problem as a knob you can turn to get different results. The Fibonacci numbers in Chapter 4, for instance, started out as an answer to a counting problem about how many rabbits there will be after *n* generations, given some constraints about how the rabbits reproduce. Turn the knob to *n* = 6 generations and you get 8, the answer for the sixth generation. Turn the knob to *n* = 7 generations and you get 13.

Many counting problems are solved with a sequence, and once we have a sequence, we can look for patterns. We might be interested in the rate of growth of the sequence, divisibility properties, or connections with other sequences. There's a famous project that collects information about integer sequences and puts them in order, like a dictionary: the On-Line Encyclopedia of Integer Sequences® (OEIS®). It started off in the 1960s as a database stored on punched cards and maintained by Neil Sloane of AT&T Bell Labs. It's grown considerably over the years and now lives at *https://oeis.org*. The OEIS welcomes contributions of new sequences from the public, so if you come up with an interesting sequence that nobody's thought of before, you can submit it!

Climbing Mountains with Catalan Numbers

The *Catalan numbers* are a sequence of numbers that arise in various counting problems, including the one we'll look at here. Suppose you want to build a jagged path of up and down steps, like charting a path over the mountains in a mountain range. You start at ground level and move one step forward at a time, stepping either up or down. At the end, you finish back at ground level. The only restriction is that the mountain range must not dip below ground level at any point. How many different patterns of up and down steps—that is, how many unique mountain ranges—can you create?

More and more mountain ranges are possible as the number of steps grows, but there are some important limits that stem from the central constraint. Because you have to stay above ground level, the very first step you take has to be up, not down. What's more, there always have to be at least as many up steps as down steps that have been taken so far. Otherwise, if you go down more than up, you'll end up below ground level. For example, if we write an up step as ↗ and a down step as ↘, then something like ↗↘↘↗↗↘ wouldn't work. Spread it out in two dimensions to see why not:

The mountain range dips below the starting position after the first up-down, so it isn't allowed. On the other hand, the step sequence ↗↗↘↘↗↘ is allowed. It spreads out as follows:

Essentially, to end up back at ground level, the steps have to occur in pairs: for every up, there eventually has to be a corresponding down. So we can use *n* to represent just the number of up steps, and we can say that the Catalan number *C*(*n*) is the total number of acceptable paths that can be made with *n* up steps. The same *n* also represents the number of down steps, for a total of 2*n* steps in each path.

In all, there are five acceptable paths that can be built with *n* = 3 up steps and *n* = 3 down steps. In other words, *C*(3) = 5. One of those paths is the ↗↗↘↘↗↘ pattern I just showed. Can you find the others? It isn't too hard to think through all the possible combinations with a low *n* value like 3, but as *n* increases, it becomes more important to have a systematic method for keeping track of all the paths. The beauty of finding the right method is what makes combinatorics the *art* of counting.

Something that worked for the Fibonacci numbers in Chapter 4 was finding a *recurrence*, a formula that let us build new numbers in the sequence from old ones. In that case, all we had to do was add the two previous numbers together to get the next number. With Catalan numbers, we might try fitting together old paths that we've already generated to form new, longer paths, but we'll need to go back further than two terms in the sequence to find them all. In fact, we'll have to look at every shorter path we've already generated.

We can build a new path with *n* up arrows by first picking any two numbers that add up to *n* − 1. Let's call them *a* and *b*. If *n* were 3, for example, we could choose *a* = 1 and *b* = 1, or *a* = 0 and *b* = 2, or *a* = 2 and *b* = 0, since those all add up to 3 − 1 = 2. For the old paths, we know there's only one path for *a* or *b* = 0. It's an empty path with zero up steps and zero down steps, where we don't go anywhere. Likewise, there's just one path with one up arrow (for *a* or *b* = 1): ↗↘. There are two paths with two up arrows (for *a* or *b* = 2): ↗↗↘↘ and ↗↘↗↘.

The recipe for building new paths is to start with an up arrow (↗), followed by any previously created path with *a* up arrows. Then, we add a down arrow (↘), followed by any previously created path with *b* up arrows. That gives us a total of *n* up arrows: the first up arrow followed by the *n* − 1 up arrows in the two paths with *a* and *b* up arrows. The first up arrow and the constraints on the previously generated paths guarantee that the number of down arrows never exceeds the number of up arrows, which would put us below ground level.

Let's use this recipe to create every possible path for *n* = 3. For *a* = 1 and *b* = 1, we build just one path: ↗↗↘↘↗↘. For *a* = 0 and *b* = 2, there are two cases: ↗↘↗↗↘↘ and ↗↘↗↘↗↘. For *a* = 2 and *b* = 0, there are also two cases: ↗↗↗↘↘↘ and ↗↗↘↗↘↘. And that's it. Those are the five possible paths with *n* = 3 up steps.

Notice how when *a* = 0, each newly generated path is just ↗↘ followed by an older path with *b* up steps. Meanwhile, when *b* = 0, the new path is just an old path with *a* up steps jacked up so there's an extra ↗ at the beginning and an extra ↘ at the end.

Every acceptable path with *n* up steps can be generated using this simple recipe, as long as we consider every possible combination of values for *a* and *b*. For *n* = 4, for example, we would need all the values of *a* and *b* that add up to 3: 0 + 3, 1 + 2, 2 + 1, and 3 + 0.

Project 28: Navigating Catalan Paths

In this project we'll write a Scratch program to build new Catalan paths using the approach we just discussed. First, we need to classify paths by how many up steps they have, so we define a block (shown in Figure 7-1) that counts all the up steps in a sequence.

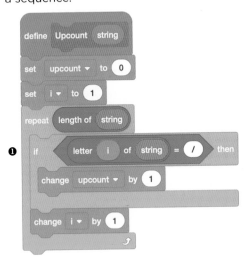

Figure 7-1: How many up steps?

This block assumes that each path is expressed as a string, with a forward slash character (/) to represent a step up and a backslash character (\) to represent a step down. The block scans the string character by character. Each time it finds a forward slash ❶, it increases the upcount variable by 1.

We can now build a list called Catalan containing all the acceptable paths up to a desired number of up steps. We start with a path of length 0 and then repeatedly apply the recurrence to get longer and longer new paths. The main program in Figure 7-2 just asks the user how far to go and then calls the custom Iterate block ❶ the right number of times.

Figure 7-2: Listing all the paths

The real work is in the Iterate block, shown in Figure 7-3, which performs the recurrence.

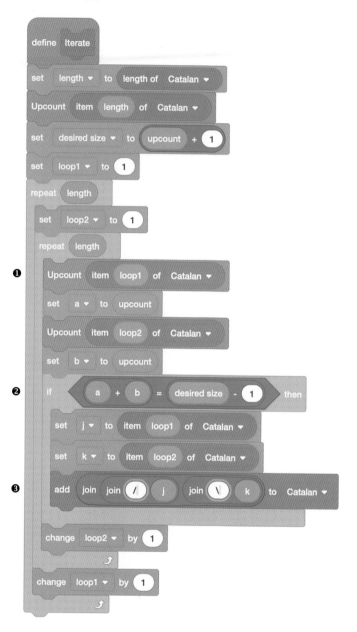

Figure 7-3: Making new paths from old paths

We use two nested loops to look at all pairs of paths that have been generated so far. Each path in the pair is classified by its number of up steps. For example, Upcount item loop1 of Catalan gives us the upcount of the first path in the pair ❶. Every time we find two paths that together have the correct number of up steps ❷, we combine them with an extra up and down step ❸ (notice the extra space after the / and \ characters, which makes the spacing of the output nicer) and add the resulting new path to Catalan. The code is written so the condition for building a new Catalan path is a + b = desired size - 1. That way, when we add the extra up step and down step, we get a path with desired size up steps.

The Results

As usual, the output is constrained by the Scratch stage, but you can scroll to see more output or export the Catalan list as a text file to see the complete contents. Figure 7-4 shows the top of the list.

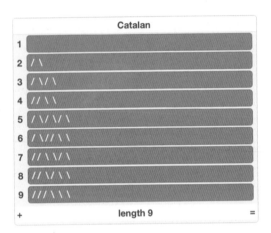

Figure 7-4: Catalan paths for n = 0, 1, 2, and 3

The first item shows the initial empty path, which grows into a path of ╱╲ when the recurrence is applied the first time. The figure includes the output through *n* = 3, showing the five acceptable paths with three up steps (list items 5 through 9). Figure 7-5 shows the next few paths in exported text format, corresponding to *n* = 4.

```
10    / \ / \ / \ / \
11    / \ / \ / / \ \
12    / \ / / \ \ / \
13    / \ / / \ / \ \
14    / \ / / / \ \ \
15    / / \ \ / \ / \
16    / / \ \ / / \ \
17    / / \ / \ \ / \
18    / / / \ \ \ / \
19    / / \ / \ / \ \
20    / / \ / / \ \ \
21    / / / \ \ / \ \
22    / / / \ / \ \ \
23    / / / / \ \ \ \
```

Figure 7-5: Catalan paths for n = 4

Scratch's list length limit of 200,000 means that this program works only up to $n = 11$, when 58,786 new paths are generated and added to the list containing the 23,714 shorter paths for values of n from 0 to 10. There are too many paths for $n = 12$ to complete the list any further. Worse, the double loop in the Iterate block takes a long time to complete. Since every pair of paths is screened to see if they join to satisfy the Catalan condition, there are as many pairs of paths to test as the square of the length of the list so far. There's a definite lag by the time we get to $n = 10$ or 11.

Still, by counting up the items in the list with a given number of steps, we can begin to see the sequence of Catalan numbers using this program. Starting with $C(0) = C(1) = 1$, the next several values in the sequence are 2, 5, 14, 42, 132, 429, 1,430, 4,862, 16,796, and 58,786.

Hacking the Code

If we want to know only the Catalan numbers themselves—that is, how many unique paths there are for each value of n—we don't have to go through the trouble of actually constructing all the paths. Instead, we can calculate the numbers directly using a recurrence based on the same combinatorial insight that helped us generate new paths. To find $C(n)$, we first need to find all the pairs of values a and b such that $a + b = n - 1$. Then, for each pair, we can look up the corresponding Catalan numbers and multiply them together: $C(a) \cdot C(b)$. Finally, we add all those products up to get $C(n)$.

For example, say we want to find $C(5)$. Since $5 - 1 = 4$, we first need to find all the pairs of numbers that add up to 4. They are $0 + 4$, $1 + 3$, $2 + 2$, $3 + 1$, and $4 + 0$. Notice how the first value in each pair is counting up from 0 to $n - 1$, while the second value is counting down. Next, we need the Catalan numbers corresponding to the values in these pairs. Assuming we've been using this recurrence to calculate all the Catalan numbers starting from $C(0)$, we should know them already: $C(0) = 1$, $C(1) = 1$, $C(2) = 2$, $C(3) = 5$, and $C(4) = 14$. We can then multiply each pair of Catalan numbers and add the results together to get $C(5)$:

$$C(5) = C(0)C(4) + C(1)C(3) + C(2)C(2) + C(3)C(1) + C(4)C(0)$$
$$= (1 \cdot 14) + (1 \cdot 5) + (2 \cdot 2) + (5 \cdot 1) + (14 \cdot 1)$$
$$= 14 + 5 + 4 + 5 + 14$$
$$= 42$$

A short way to write this recurrence formula is to use summation notation, where a Σ symbol (the uppercase Greek letter sigma) indicates an addition of one term for each value of the index i from the smallest value of $i = 0$ (indicated below the Σ) to the largest value of $i = n - 1$ (indicated above the Σ):

$$C(n) = \sum_{i=0}^{n-1} C(i)C(n - 1 - i)$$

Here, i is equivalent to a, and $n - 1 - i$ is equivalent to b. This makes sense; if $a + b = n - 1$, then $b = n - 1 - a$.

Figure 7-6 shows some code to have Scratch calculate and list as many Catalan numbers as we want.

Figure 7-6: Making a list of Catalan numbers

We name the list C(n) and start by adding 1 to it for $C(0) = 1$. It would be much better, though, if the list indices matched the indices of the sequence entries, with index 1 holding $C(1)$, index 2 holding $C(2)$, and so on. To make this happen, we delete the first item from the list at the end of the program ❶.

As in the original Catalan program, the actual work is done in an Iterate block, which we can call as many times as we want. Figure 7-7 shows the block definition.

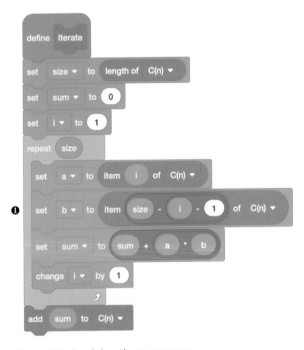

Figure 7-7: Applying the recurrence

Inside a repeat loop, we look up pairs of Catalan numbers, with the value of the variable a starting at i(1) and increasing up to size while the value of the variable b starts at size and decreases, to account for all pairs in the recurrence. Notice how the definition of b makes it count backward ❶. We multiply each pair of values and add them to the running total being kept in the sum variable, which is added to the list at the end of the block.

With the recurrence, Scratch is able to calculate the values of $C(n)$ quite quickly, and the limiting value of the program is determined by flintmax instead of the maximum list length. The results are accurate until flintmax is exceeded, which happens after $n = 30$. The value Scratch calculates for $C(31)$ is off by 1. We don't exceed Scratch's floating-point maximum and start getting answers of Infinity, however, until we hit $n = 520$.

Programming Challenges

7.1 Here's another recurrence for Catalan numbers:

$$C(n) = \frac{2(2n - 1)}{n + 1} C(n - 1)$$

After starting with $C(0) = 1$, this formula applies to all values of n greater than 0. Program this alternative Catalan recurrence in Scratch.

7.2 Write a program to make Scratch draw the up-down mountains when you provide a path from a row of the Catalan list.

7.3 There's a relationship between the Catalan numbers and the central binomial coefficients in Pascal's triangle, which are entries of the form $C(2n, n)$. Calculate some central binomial coefficients using the program from Project 19 (Figure 5-7), and see if you can find another formula for calculating Catalan numbers.

7.4 Another counting problem where Catalan numbers arise involves specifying the order of multiplication by nesting parentheses. Think about how you might multiply four numbers a, b, c, and d by changing how they're grouped via parentheses, instead of changing the order of the factors. For example, $((ab)c)d$ would first multiply a and b, then multiply the result of that calculation (the *partial product*) by c, and finally multiply that by d. On the other hand, $(ab)(cd)$ first multiplies a and b, then multiplies c and d, and finally multiplies together the two partial products. There are three more ways to group four numbers. Find them. Then, change the program for generating Catalan paths so it shows all the ways the parentheses could be grouped.

Breaking Down Numbers with Addition

Many of the questions we've explored about numbers in earlier chapters have been about multiplication. For example, the prime numbers are multiplicative building blocks of the positive integers, and the fundamental theorem of arithmetic says there's only one way to write a number as a product of primes (ignoring the order of the factors, that is). But what about addition? What are some ways we can write a number as the sum of other numbers?

For starters, we might focus on the number 1 and note that every positive integer can be written uniquely as a sum of 1s: $2 = 1 + 1$, $3 = 1 + 1 + 1$, and so on. We could also impose a different restriction and require that each *summand* (a number being added) be used at most once. Then, there's a unique representation for every positive integer if we think in base 2. That is, every positive integer can be uniquely expressed as a sum of distinct powers of 2. (We explored binary representations in Chapter 1.) For example, the only way to get 5 without reusing the same power of 2 is $2^2 + 2^0$, or $4 + 1$. As soon as we allow a larger set of possible summands than the powers of 2, however, we lose uniqueness. If we permit 3 as a summand along with the powers of 2, for instance, we can get 5 using $1 + 4$ or $2 + 3$.

Compositions: Order Does Matter

Another decision to make is whether order should matter. Do we count $1 + 2$ and $2 + 1$ as different representations of 3? If we decide they should be considered different, then there's an easy way to find the number of possible representations of a given number n as a sum (also called the *compositions* of n). First, write $n = 1 + 1 + \ldots + 1$. Then, look at each plus sign and make a choice: either keep it or omit it and combine the numbers on each side of it. For example, say $n = 3$. We could take $3 = 1 + 1 + 1$ and decide to get rid of either the first plus sign, making $3 = 11 + 1 \rightarrow 2 + 1$, or the second plus sign, making $3 = 1 + 11 \rightarrow 1 + 2$. We can also keep both plus signs and get $1 + 1 + 1$, or get rid of both and get the single summand 3.

We've found four compositions of 3, and that's all there are. To see why, and to develop a general formula for the number of compositions of n, think about the process of going from $1 + 1 + 1 + \ldots + 1$ to a composition of n. A string of n 1s have $n - 1$ plus signs between them. For each plus sign, we have a binary choice to make: keep it or drop it. That means there are $n - 1$ independent binary decisions, which works out to 2^{n-1} ways to combine the decisions and make a composition of n. The four compositions of 3 that we identified are "drop, keep," "keep, drop," "keep, keep," and "drop, drop."

Partitions: Order Doesn't Matter

A more interesting situation, and one that doesn't have an answer with such an easy formula, is if we decide that the order of summands *doesn't* matter—for example, that $1 + 2$ and $2 + 1$ should be treated as the same representation of 3. Such a representation, where we ignore the order, is called a *partition* of n rather than a composition.

If the order of summands doesn't matter, we might as well put the summands in increasing (or rather, nondecreasing) order so we can keep track of all the partitions in a more systematic way. We can then think of a partition as a special kind of composition whose terms are nondecreasing. For example, the three partitions of 3 are 1 + 1 + 1, 1 + 2, and 3.

NOTE   *I say* nondecreasing *rather than* increasing *because it wouldn't really be fair to think of the 1s in 1 + 1 + 1 as being in increasing order. The important thing is that the value of each summand isn't less than the previous one.*

Let's call $P(n)$ the function that counts the number of partitions of n. Make sure you agree that $P(1) = 1$ (there's only one partition of 1: 1 = 1) and that $P(2) = 2$ (2 = 1 + 1, 2 = 2). We've already determined that there are three partitions of 3, so $P(3) = 3$. You might think you see a pattern, but the number of partitions of n starts to grow more quickly from here on: $P(4) = 5$, $P(5) = 7$, and by the time we get to 12 we have $P(12) = 77$.

Project 29: A Partition Expedition

Let's develop a Scratch program to find all the partitions for a given value of n. We'll store the results in a partitions list, with each partition represented as a string of numbers separated by plus signs without any spaces in between, such as 1+1+2. Our strategy will be to start at $n = 1$ and work our way up to the desired value of n, replacing the contents of partitions with the current n's partitions every step of the way. This means we need a way to use a list of all the partitions of n to find all the partitions of $n + 1$.

Some partitions of $n + 1$ are available by adding a summand of 1 to the start of each partition of n. This is just a matter of joining 1+ to each item in the partitions list. Figure 7-8 shows a custom block to do that.

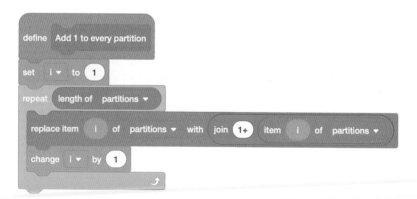

Figure 7-8: Building new partitions from old partitions

This block simply cycles through the partitions list, taking one item at a time, adding 1+ to the beginning of it, and storing the result back in the same position in the list.

The remaining partitions of $n + 1$ can be built by looking back at the partitions of $n - 1$ and adding a new first term of 2, looking back at the partitions of $n - 2$ and adding a new first term of 3, and so on. This step is a little trickier since, because of the nondecreasing order rule, not every newly created partition will be acceptable. For example, the only partitions of $n - 1$ that can have a 2 added to them are the ones that had a smallest term of at least 2 to begin with. If there's a 1 in the partition, putting a 2 in front breaks the order. Similarly, when adding a 3 to a partition of $n - 2$, the original partition can't begin with a 1 or a 2.

Another complication is that the partitions list in our program holds only the partitions of n, which are modified to become the partitions of $n + 1$. We don't actually have a record of the earlier partitions of $n - 1$, $n - 2$, and so on to look back at. There's a workaround, though: once we've taken all the partitions of n and added a 1 at the beginning to make partitions of $n + 1$, we can look at each new partition and combine all the 1s. If there are two 1s, this will have the same effect as adding a 2 to the partitions of $n - 1$. Similarly, if there are three, it will be equivalent to adding a 3 to partitions of $n - 2$, and so on.

To see why this works, consider the case of going from $n = 5$ to $n + 1 = 6$. One partition of 5 is $1 + 2 + 2$, and adding an extra 1 to it gives us $1 + 1 + 2 + 2$, a partition of 6. If we combine those 1s into a 2, we get $2 + 2 + 2$, another partition of 6. This is the equivalent of looking back at the partitions of $n - 1 = 4$, finding the partition $2 + 2$, and adding a 2 in front of it. Likewise, another partition of 5 is $1 + 1 + 3$. Adding an extra 1 gives us $1 + 1 + 1 + 3 = 6$. If we combine those 1s into a 3, we get $3 + 3$, the same as if we'd looked back at the partitions of $n - 2 = 3$, found the partition 3 (any number is a valid partition of itself), and added a 3 in front of it.

Implementing this process in code takes a few steps. First, we need to copy the contents of partitions (the partitions of $n + 1$ that we got by adding an initial term of 1 to the old partitions of n) into a new list so we don't overwrite them. The block in Figure 7-9 does this, placing the copy in a list called dup.

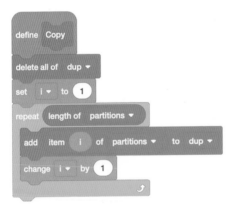

Figure 7-9: Copying the list of partitions
to a duplicate list

Next, we need a way to count how many 1s there are at the start of a given partition. The block in Figure 7-10 handles this task.

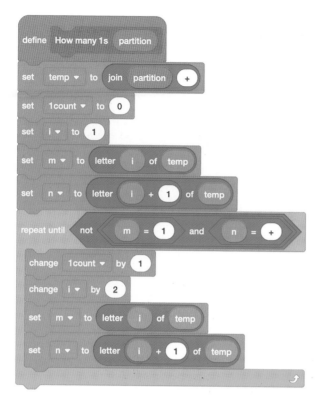

Figure 7-10: Counting the number of 1s in a partition

Remember, we're assuming that each partition is a string of numbers separated by plus signs, but we don't know how many digits each number contains. So this How many 1s block looks at the string two characters at a time and checks if the first character (m) is a 1 and the second (n) is a plus sign. The repeat until loop keeps incrementing 1count until this is no longer the case. Checking for the plus sign as well as the 1 prevents a string like 1+10 from being counted as two 1s. Notice also that we temporarily add an extra plus sign to the end of the string at the start of the block. Without this, the final 1 in a string of all 1s (like 1+1+1) wouldn't be counted.

Once we have the number of 1s in the 1count variable, we can replace all those 1s with the value in 1count. The block in Figure 7-11 makes the replacement. This block also makes the initial call to the How many 1s block.

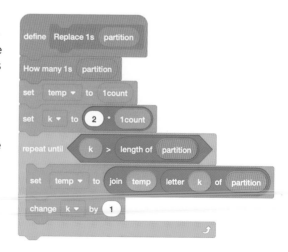

Figure 7-11: Combining the 1s into a larger number

In this block, we build up the new partition in the temp variable. We start by setting temp to 1count. Then, we use the index variable k to copy the rest of the original partition string into temp, starting from character 2 * 1count, which is the plus sign after the last 1. If the original partition consisted entirely of 1s, the k > length of partition test for the repeat until loop will fail immediately, so the new partition will just be the value of 1count.

Now comes the real work: we need to decide if the string we've created by replacing some initial 1s with a single larger number qualifies as a proper partition and should be added to the partitions list. There are two things that matter here. First, the first term can't be a 1. If it is, it's already been counted. (This will be the case if the original partition had only a single 1, in which case the Replace 1s block will have left it unchanged.) Second, the string of numbers must be in nondecreasing order. We know the original partition was in nondecreasing order, and all we've done is combine all the 1s into a larger number, so the only way this condition can fail is if the new first term is bigger than the second term. There's also the possibility that the partition consists of a single term. This should be considered proper as well. The block in Figure 7-12 tests for all of these cases.

This block is designed to set the proper variable to a Boolean value, true or false, depending on whether the string p represents a proper partition. We start with a repeat until loop that extracts the first number into the first variable ❶. The loop continues until the index variable i encounters a plus sign or goes beyond the length of the string. We need this loop because the number may have multiple digits. At this point, if i has exceeded the length of the whole string ❷, we know the partition contains a single term, so we set proper to true.

If we haven't reached the end of the string, we use another repeat until loop to extract the second number into the second variable ❸. (Again, it could have multiple digits.) We then perform our two main checks again: if first is greater than second or if first is 1 ❹, we set proper to false. Otherwise, we have a valid partition, so we set proper to true.

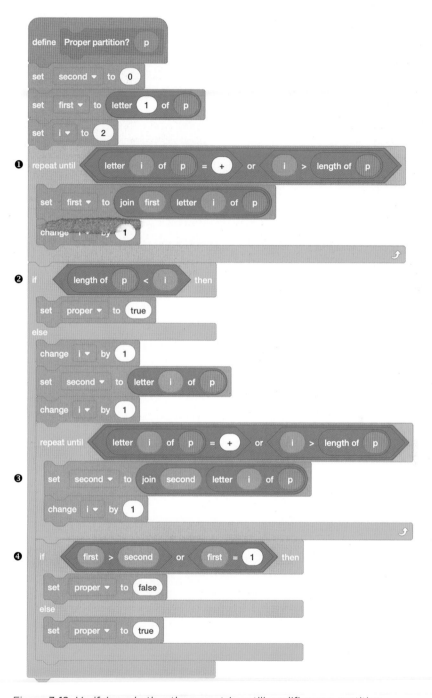

Figure 7-12: Verifying whether the new string still qualifies as a partition

With all the blocks we've defined so far, we can now define a main Iterate block that coordinates the process of building the next batch of partitions from the previous batch. Figure 7-13 shows how.

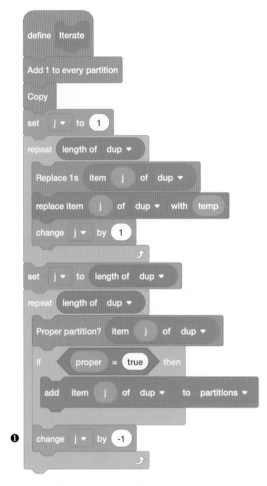

Figure 7-13: Growing the list of partitions from
n to n + 1

This block almost reads like a verbal description of the algorithm. First, we add 1 to every existing partition and make a copy of the partitions list. Next, we take each partition in the copy and combine all its 1s into a single summand. We then evaluate the results, adding only the proper ones to the partitions list.

During the evaluation phase, notice that we use the counter j to move backward through the dup list ❶. A quirk of the algorithm is that because of the way partitions are added to this list, the results end up being generated from highest number first to lowest number first. For example, 1 + 1 + 1 + 1 = 4 initially comes before 1 + 1 + 2 = 4, but after these are transformed into 4 and 2 + 2, the 4 is listed first. Evaluating the list in reverse puts the results back into ascending order.

Now that we have all the pieces in place, we just need the green flag code in Figure 7-14 to set the program in motion.

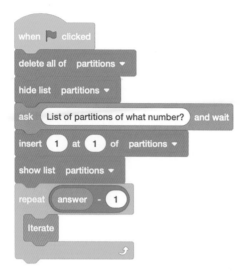

Figure 7-14: Generating a list of partitions

This stack prompts for a number and iterates enough times to get the partitions of that number. We start off the partitions list with just a 1, the only viable partition of 1 itself.

The Results

Figure 7-15 shows the output of a sample run of the program: a list of all 11 partitions of the number 6.

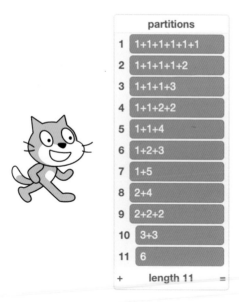

	partitions
1	1+1+1+1+1+1
2	1+1+1+1+2
3	1+1+1+3
4	1+1+2+2
5	1+1+4
6	1+2+3
7	1+5
8	2+4
9	2+2+2
10	3+3
11	6
+	length 11 =

Figure 7-15: Partitions of 6

As usual, to see the whole list for larger values of *n*, you'll need to either scroll down or export the list to a text file.

Hacking the Code

We can calculate $P(n)$, the number of partitions of n, by having Scratch list them all and then seeing how long the list is. This works as long as the list can hold all of the partitions. Scratch's limit on list length means this program works for values of n up to 49, which has 173,525 partitions. (On my nine-year-old computer, it takes less than two minutes to find them all.) For higher values of n, we can use a recurrence formula to calculate $P(n)$ directly, without having to list all the partitions. It turns out that the recurrence represents $P(n)$ as a combination of earlier terms that are spaced out in an interesting way. The relation is:

$$P(n) = P(n - 1) + P(n - 2)$$
$$- P(n - 5) - P(n - 7)$$
$$+ P(n - 12) + P(n - 15)$$
$$- P(n - 22) - P(n - 26)$$
$$+ \ldots$$

The sequence 1, 5, 12, 22, ..., running down the left column, is the sequence of pentagonal numbers from Chapter 4, given as follows:

$$\frac{k(3k - 1)}{2} \text{ for } k = 1, 2, 3, \ldots$$

The related sequence 2, 7, 15, 26, ..., running down the right column, is calculated like this:

$$\frac{k(3k + 1)}{2} \text{ for } k = 1, 2, 3, \ldots$$

The second sequence could also be written as follows to see a different kind of symmetry:

$$\frac{k(3k - 1)}{2} \text{ for } k = -1, -2, -3, \ldots$$

Take a look back at Figure 4-14 in Project 16 on page 71 to see both of these sequences highlighted in the visualization of the pentagonal numbers.

We can program this recurrence in Scratch to take the calculation of values of $P(n)$ much further. First, we need the custom blocks in Figure 7-16 to calculate values for the two sequences just described, given a certain value of k.

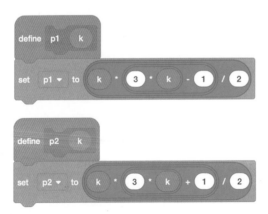

Figure 7-16: Formulas for calculating pentagonal numbers

Next, Figure 7-17 shows an `Initialize` block that sets up `Partitions`, a list for storing the results.

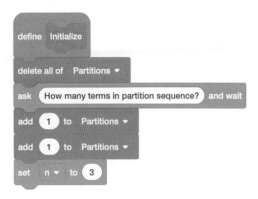

Figure 7-17: Initializing the recurrence

We ask how many values of $P(n)$ to calculate and seed the list with the first two values, $P(0) = 1$ and $P(1) = 1$. We then set n to 3 to start calculating at the third term of the sequence, the value for $P(2)$.

The main program stack, shown in Figure 7-18, calls `Initialize` and then uses a repeat loop to calculate the desired number of values of $P(n)$.

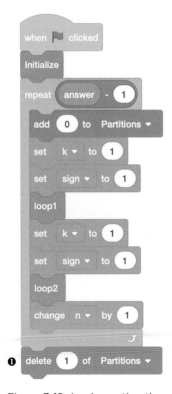

Figure 7-18: Implementing the recurrence for the partition function

We start each new $P(n)$ value at 0 and use two custom blocks, loop1 and loop2, to calculate the actual value using the recurrence formula, starting from $k = 1$. Once the repeat loop is over, we remove the first item, representing $P(0)$, from the Partitions list so the index numbers match the values of n ❶.

Figure 7-19 shows the definitions of loop1 and loop2.

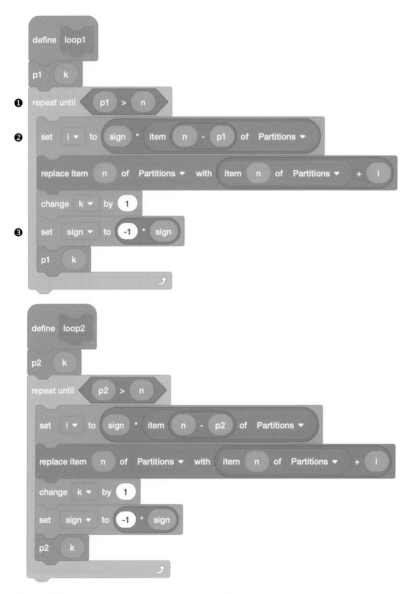

Figure 7-19: Loops to calculate pentagonal numbers

In loop1, we look up earlier values from the Partitions list according to the left column of the recurrence rule—that is, $P(n - 1)$, $P(n - 5)$, $P(n - 12)$, and so on—using the p1 block to calculate the necessary pentagonal numbers. Each value is stored in the variable i and then added to the latest value in Partitions. Since the terms in the recurrence alternate between addition and subtraction, we use the sign variable ❷ to keep track of which operation is needed. It started as 1 (addition) before loop1 was called in Figure 7-18, and for each new term we multiply it by -1 to switch from addition to subtraction or vice versa ❸. We continue looking up terms until the next pentagonal number (p1) is greater than the current value of n ❶.

The loop2 block follows the same logic, but it uses p2 to calculate terms from the right column of the recurrence rule: $P(n - 2)$, $P(n - 7)$, $P(n - 15)$, and so on.

Figure 7-20 shows some sample output from this program.

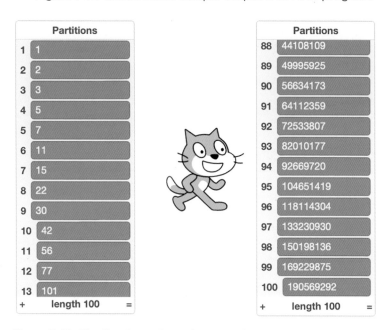

Figure 7-20: The first few values of P(n), and some later ones

This approach rapidly produces correct values for $P(n)$ through $n = 298$, until the numbers being combined in the recurrence exceed flintmax. As n continues to grow, the limitations of floating-point arithmetic make the calculated values of $P(n)$ unreliable, oscillating wildly through incorrect values and even some negative numbers before the floating-point limit is reached and we get Infinity.

Programming Challenges

7.5 We can come up with interesting counting problems for partitions by putting extra conditions on the summands. Write a Boolean block that

(continued)

screens partitions and returns true if every summand is an odd number. Apply the block to the list of partitions generated for a given value of *n* using the code in Figure 7-14 and see how many have this property. For example, the partitions of 5 with all odd summands would be 1 + 1 + 1 + 1 + 1, 1 + 1 + 3, and 5 itself.

7.6 Write another Boolean block to check if all the parts of a partition are distinct. For example, the partitions of 5 with all distinct parts would be 1 + 4, 2 + 3, and 5 itself. The partition 1 + 2 + 2, among others, wouldn't count, since it has a repeated part. Compare the number of partitions of *n* with distinct parts with the number of partitions of *n* with all odd parts.

7.7 The Indian mathematician Srinivasa Ramanujan noticed that *P(n)* is divisible by 5 whenever *n* ends in 4 or 9. Verify that fact from a list of *P(n)* values. Remember that you can export a Scratch list as a text file to view it more easily. See if you can find other patterns for values of *P(n)* that are divisible by 7 and 11.

Conclusion

We've seen in earlier chapters that Scratch is good for calculating numbers and processing text. Now we know it's also good for making patterns. Sometimes the first step in counting how many ways a pattern can occur is just making a list of what's possible—one more job for Scratch Cat! Then, with the right formula or recurrence, we can count the occurrences of a pattern without actually having to list them all.

8

Three Helpings of Pi

The number π (pi) represents the ratio of a circle's circumference (the distance all the way around the circle's "rim") to its diameter (the straight line distance from one side of the circle through its center to the other side). Remarkably, the value of this ratio is the same no matter what size the circle is. Other properties of a circle, like its area, depend on its size, but not π; as the size of the circle increases, the ratio of the increasing circumference to the increasing diameter remains constant.

You can think of measurements of circumference and diameter as being given in a common length unit, like centimeters or inches. In the ratio, the units of these measurements cancel out, leaving π as a pure number, dimensionless. It's often approximated as 3.14, but the digits beyond the decimal point actually continue on forever, without repeating. Over the years, mathematicians have devised lots of different ways to calculate π, with varying degrees of accuracy. In this chapter, we'll consider a few such techniques, using algebra, geometry, and even number theory.

How Archimedes Calculated Pi

Let's first explore an approach to calculating π used by the ancient Greek mathematician Archimedes. Start by drawing a circle, then draw an *inscribed* polygon, a shape that fits completely inside the circle with its corners just touching the circle's rim. Next, draw a *circumscribed* polygon, a shape that completely surrounds the circle such that the midpoint of each side touches the rim of the circle. The two polygons should have the same number of sides, and they should be *regular* polygons, meaning all their sides are of equal length. Figure 8-1 shows what this drawing might look like.

Notice that the perimeter of the inscribed (purple) hexagon is smaller than the circumference of the circle, and the perimeter of the circumscribed (black) hexagon is larger than the circumference of the circle. This means we can use the perimeters of these two hexagons to find lower and upper bounds for the value of π.

Figure 8-1: Inscribed and circumscribed hexagons

The figure doesn't specify length units, so let's say the circle has a radius of $r = 1$. A circle with a radius of 1 is called a *unit circle*. This unit circle has a circumference of $C = 2\pi r = 2\pi$. The inscribed hexagon is made up of six equilateral triangles with side length 1, so by summing the lengths of the outer edges of the triangles we can determine that the size of the perimeter of the inscribed hexagon is 6. This in turn tells us that $2\pi > 6$, so $\pi > 3$.

With a little bit of trigonometry, we can calculate that the circumscribed hexagon has sides of length $(2\sqrt{3}) / 3$, so the size of its perimeter is $(6 \cdot 2\sqrt{3}) / 3$. This equals $4\sqrt{3}$, and if $2\pi < 4\sqrt{3}$, then $\pi < 2\sqrt{3}$, or approximately 3.4642.

We now know that π is between 3 and 3.4642. To get a little more precision, let's try doubling the number of sides of the inscribed and circumscribed polygons. As the number of sides increases, the inner and outer polygons nestle closer to the circle. Figure 8-2 shows what happens when we go from 6 sides to 12, for example.

As the polygons get closer and closer to the circle, their perimeters *converge* on the value of 2π. Archimedes went from 6- to 12- to 24- to 48- to 96-sided polygons and reached an approximation for π that was the best known for centuries: $223 / 71 < \pi < 22 / 7$.

Figure 8-2: Inscribed and circumscribed 12-sided polygons

Archimedes arrived at his approximation by developing a recurrence rule for tracking how the perimeters change when you double the number of sides of the two polygons. The recurrence takes a_n and b_n, the old upper and lower bounds of π, and calculates the new upper and lower bounds after the doubling, a_{n+1} and b_{n+1}, as follows:

$$a_{n+1} = \frac{2a_n b_n}{a_n + b_n}$$

$$b_{n+1} = \sqrt{a_{n+1} b_n}$$

For example, to go from our initial hexagons, where $a_1 = 2\sqrt{3}$ and $b_1 = 3$, to the 12-sided polygons, we calculate

$$a_2 = \frac{2a_1b_1}{a_1 + b_1} = \frac{2 \cdot 2\sqrt{3} \cdot 3}{2\sqrt{3} + 3} \approx 3.21539$$

and:

$$b_2 = \sqrt{a_2b_1} = \sqrt{\frac{2 \cdot 2\sqrt{3} \cdot 3}{2\sqrt{3} + 3} \cdot 3} \approx 3.10583$$

This tells us that π must be between 3.10583 and 3.21539.

The calculation for a_{n+1} is called the *harmonic mean* of a_n and b_n. The calculation for b_{n+1} is the *geometric mean* of a_{n+1} and b_n. You can find more details about what these terms mean and how Archimedes used trigonometry to derive his recurrence at *https://mathworld.wolfram.com/ArchimedesRecurrenceFormula.html*.

Project 30: Archimedes's Recurrence

In this project, we'll program Archimedes's recurrence in Scratch in order to calculate an approximation of π. We'll start with hexagons, which, as we've established, give an upper bound a_1 of $2\sqrt{3}$ and a lower bound b_1 of 3. Then, we'll have the number of sides double from there. Figure 8-3 shows the code.

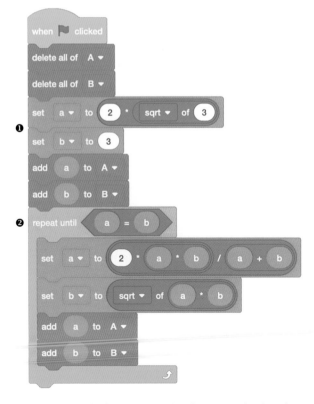

Figure 8-3: Calculating π starting from inscribed and circumscribed hexagons

After setting the starting values for the upper and lower bounds ❶, we use a loop to calculate new values until the results are equal ❷, meaning we've reached the highest level of accuracy that Scratch can support. We store the upper bounds in list A and the lower bounds in list B. In the loop, notice how we calculate the new value of a first so we can use it in our calculation of b.

The Results

Figure 8-4 shows the contents of the A and B lists after running the program.

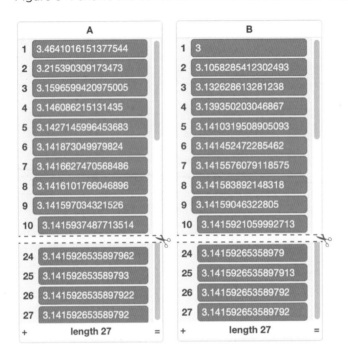

	A		B
1	3.4641016151377544	1	3
2	3.215390309173473	2	3.1058285412302493
3	3.1596599420975005	3	3.132628613281238
4	3.146086215131435	4	3.139350203046867
5	3.1427145996453683	5	3.1410319508905093
6	3.141873049979824	6	3.141452472285462
7	3.1416627470568486	7	3.1415576079118575
8	3.1416101766046896	8	3.141583892148318
9	3.141597034321526	9	3.14159046322805
10	3.1415937487713514	10	3.1415921059992713
24	3.1415926535897962	24	3.14159265358979
25	3.141592653589793	25	3.1415926535897913
26	3.1415926535897922	26	3.141592653589792
27	3.141592653589792	27	3.141592653589792
+	length 27 =	+	length 27 =

Figure 8-4: Starting with hexagons and converging to π

It takes just 27 cycles of the loop for us to hit the accuracy limits of Scratch's floating-point representation. At this point, the values of the bounds converge on 3.141592653589792. You can check that the first several digits are right if you remember the mnemonic "How I need a shake, chocolate of course, after the heavy lectures involving quantum mechanics." Count the letters in each word to get the first 15 digits of π: "How I need" is 3, 1, 4, and so on.

Hacking the Code

The side-doubling recurrence works even if we don't start with hexagons. Suppose we approximate the circumference of a circle with inscribed and circumscribed squares, as in Figure 8-5.

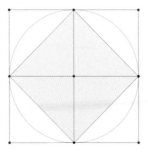

Figure 8-5: Using squares to approximate circumference

If the circle still has a radius of 1, the outer square has a perimeter of 8. By the Pythagorean theorem, the inner square has sides of length $\sqrt{2}$. Since the circle has a circumference of 2π, the first estimate is therefore $2\sqrt{2} < \pi < 4$. To run the recurrence from there, just replace the two blocks setting the initial values of a and b (see Figure 8-3 ❶ on page 153) with the blocks in Figure 8-6.

Figure 8-6: New initial values for the recurrence

Figure 8-7 shows the result of running the program with these new starting values.

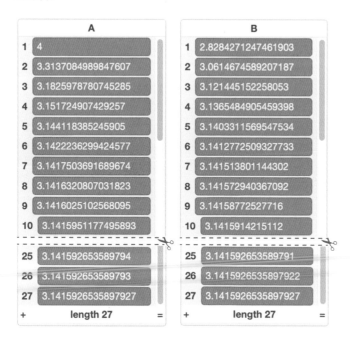

A		B	
1	4	1	2.8284271247461903
2	3.3137084989847607	2	3.0614674589207187
3	3.1825978780745285	3	3.121445152258053
4	3.151724907429257	4	3.1365484905459398
5	3.144118385245905	5	3.1403311569547534
6	3.1422236299424577	6	3.1412772509327733
7	3.1417503691689674	7	3.141513801144302
8	3.1416320807031823	8	3.141572940367092
9	3.1416025102568095	9	3.14158772527716
10	3.1415951177495893	10	3.1415914215112
25	3.141592653589794	25	3.141592653589791
26	3.141592653589793	26	3.1415926535897922
27	3.1415926535897927	27	3.1415926535897927
+	length 27 =	+	length 27 =

Figure 8-7: Starting with squares and converging to π

Even though the recurrence starts with wider bounds, it quickly converges, once again taking 27 cycles to hit Scratch's accuracy limit.

Programming Challenge

8.1 Figure out the initial values for the recurrence if you start with in-scribed and circumscribed triangles. Since the first doubling of sides goes from triangles to hexagons, the output from the second line on should be the same as in Figure 8-4.

Estimating Pi from the Area of a Circle

Another way to calculate π is to use $A = \pi r^2$, the formula for the area of a circle. Imagine you've drawn a circle with a radius of r on top of a grid, with its center at point $(0, 0)$. Any point (x, y) inside the circle will satisfy the inequality $x^2 + y^2 < r^2$. Say we focus only on points whose coordinates are integers. These are known as *lattice points*. We can think of each lattice point as the lower-left corner of a *unit square*, a square with a side length $s = 1$ and area $s^2 = 1$. Counting the number of lattice points inside the circle (the ones that satisfy the $x^2 + y^2 < r^2$ inequality) gives us an approximation of the area of the circle. Figure 8-8 shows an example of how this works, for a circle with a radius of 4.

The lattice points inside the circle are shown as purple dots. There are 45 in all. Each lattice point marks the lower-left corner of a yellow unit square. A few of these squares extend beyond the circle, but this is offset by the parts of the circle that the squares don't cover. On balance, we can say that the circle has an approx-imate area of 45, the same as the area covered by the yellow squares. We know the area of a circle is πr^2, so dividing 45 by r^2 gives us an estimated value for π: $45 / 16 = 2.8125$.

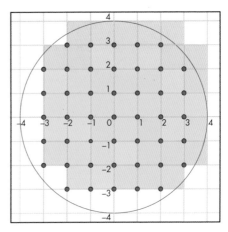

Figure 8-8: Lattice points in a circle with a radius of 4

If we also count the four lattice points that fall directly on the perimeter of the circle—points $(4, 0)$, $(0, 4)$, $(-4, 0)$, and $(-4, 0)$—we can get a better approxima-tion: $49 / 16 = 3.0625$. We could get even closer by using a bigger circle. This is because the area of the circle grows in proportion to the square of the radius, but the error comes only from the squares around the circumference, the number of which grows only in proportion to the first power of the radius. So the bigger the circle is, the less the error is relative to the overall area. In our next project, we'll see how much we can improve our estimate by increasing the size of the radius, with Scratch handling the calculations for us.

Project 31: Using the Lattice Point Tally

Figure 8-9 shows some Scratch code that prompts for a radius and counts lattice points in the resulting circle to approximate π. The output keeps track of both the number of lattice points that satisfy the condition $x^2 + y^2 < r^2$ and the resulting estimated value of π.

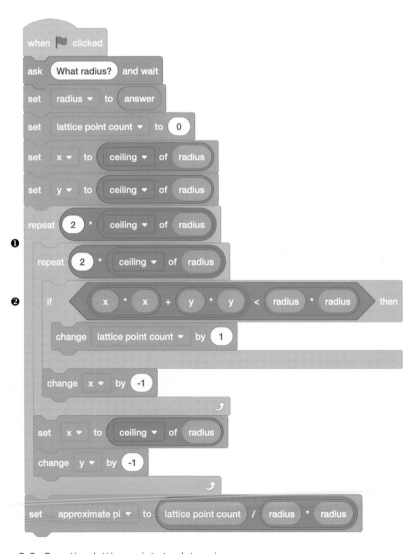

Figure 8-9: Counting lattice points to determine π

We first ask for a value for the circle's radius. Then, we use two nested loops ❶ to step through the rows and columns of lattice points in a square circumscribed around the circle. We start in the top-right corner of the square, where x and y both equal the radius *r*, and work toward the bottom-left corner, where they equal –*r*. For each pair of coordinates, we check if the point is in the circle ❷ and increment the lattice count if it is. At the end, we divide the lattice count by the square of the radius to get the approximation of π.

The Results

Figure 8-10 shows the result of running the program for a circle with a radius of 1,000.

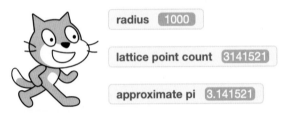

radius 1000

lattice point count 3141521

approximate pi 3.141521

Figure 8-10: Counting lattice points in a circle
with r = 1,000

This approximation of π is accurate up to the first four decimal places. Much better!

Hacking the Code

For a circle with a radius of *r*, the program in Figure 8-9 has to check $(2r)^2$ lattice points. When *r* = 1,000, that's 4 million points to check, which takes a little while. The delay gets worse as the circle gets bigger. If *r* = 10,000, for example, there will be 400 million points to check, and you'll be waiting a very long time for your results.

But why check *all* the points? We can sample a smaller number of randomly selected lattice points and use those to make a guess about the overall area of the circle. Figure 8-11 shows how.

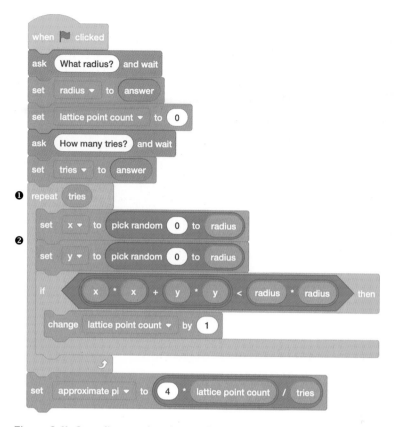

Figure 8-11: Sampling random lattice points to determine π

The variable `tries` controls the `repeat` loop ❶ and determines how many random points to check. I recommend setting it to about 10 times the radius of the circle. We can confine ourselves to looking only at points in the first quadrant of the grid, where the coordinates are positive integers, by picking random x and y values between 0 and `radius` ❷. If the point falls within the circle, we update the lattice count as before. With enough tries, we should see the following equivalence:

$$\frac{\text{hits}}{\text{total}} \approx \frac{A/4}{r^2}$$

The left side of this equivalence is the ratio of "hits" (lattice points in the circle) to the total number of points sampled. The right side is the ratio of one-fourth of the circle's area (the part of the circle in the first quadrant of the grid) to the square of its radius. Think of r^2 here as the area of the first-quadrant square containing all the points we can possibly sample. Substituting A for πr^2 and solving for π, we get:

$$\pi \approx \frac{4 \cdot \text{hits}}{\text{total}}$$

We use this equation at the end of the program to estimate π. Figure 8-12 shows an example result, with a radius of 10,000 and 100,000 randomly sampled points.

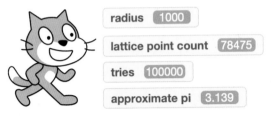

Figure 8-12: Estimating π through random trials

Your output from this program will probably be different every time you run it, since the random number generator determines the choice of points to test. Still, the result we got here is pretty close, and it's calculated much more quickly than it would have been if the program had checked every single lattice point in the circle.

Programming Challenge

8.2   There's a subtle difference between these two versions of the pick random block:

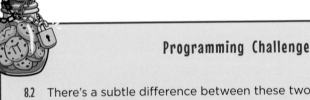

Embed each block in a little bit of code that reports the result to see how they behave. The version with 1 returns integer values, so asking for values between 0 and 1 gives 0 about half the time and 1 about half the time. The version with 1.0 returns values between 0 and 1, which aren't necessarily integers. If we don't have integer (x, y) coordinates, then we don't have true lattice points, but does that matter? See if the code in Figure 8-11 still works if the randomly chosen points don't have integer coordinates.

Approximating Pi with Relative Primes

The number π shows up in many places in mathematics that seem to be far removed from circles and geometry. One interesting formula involving π relates back to the idea of common divisors from Chapters 2 and 3. Remember that a *common divisor* of two integers is a number that's a divisor of each one. If the only common divisor that two integers have is 1, then the two integers are said to be *relatively prime*.

Here's a geometric way to interpret relative primes. Suppose you're standing at the origin of a coordinate plane, at the point (0, 0), looking out at the lattice points. You can see most of them, but some are blocked because there's another lattice point in the way. For example, Figure 8-13 marks the *visible lattice points* in the first quadrant as purple dots. The straight black lines show that the point (1, 1) blocks the points (2, 2), (3, 3), and so on; the point (2, 1) blocks (4, 2) and (6, 3); and the point (3, 2) blocks (6, 4).

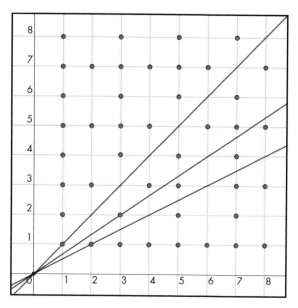

Figure 8-13: Visible and hidden lattice points

The coordinates of the visible points, such as (1, 1), (7, 2), and (3, 8), are relatively prime. The coordinates of blocked points, such as (6, 8) and (2, 4), are not. The 8×8 square shown in Figure 8-13 has 44 visible lattice points in it out of 64 points total, so the proportion that are visible is 44 / 64 ≈ 0.6875. This tells us the proportion of pairs of numbers between 1 and 8 that are relatively prime.

Now suppose we expand the size of the square. What happens to the number of visible lattice points and to the number of relatively prime pairs? Both numbers grow, of course, but in a very specific way. As the size of the square grows, the proportion of the square's lattice points that are visible approaches a limiting value of about 0.608. The amazing thing is that this number has a value related to π. It's $6/\pi^2$. The reason for this is a little too advanced for this book (if you're interested, it has to do with the Riemann zeta function), but we can still explore how the ratio behaves and use it to estimate the value of π.

Project 32: Using Only Visible Lattice Points

Let's write a program that counts the number of visible lattice points within a first-quadrant square of a given size and uses that count to calculate an approximation of π. (We're using a square here rather than a circle because it's easier to generate the points in a square with nested loops.) Since each visible point's coordinates will be relatively prime, we can use the custom gcd (greatest common divisor) block we created for Project 9 back in Chapter 2 to help (see Figure 2-17 on page 38 for the block definition). If the GCD of a set of coordinates is 1, we've found a visible lattice point. Figure 8-14 shows the code.

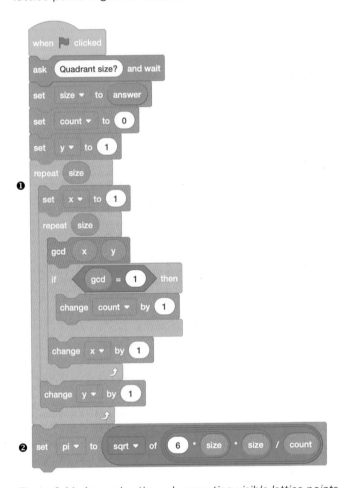

Figure 8-14: Approximating π by counting visible lattice points

We prompt for a quadrant size, then test all lattice points within the square with lower-left corner (1, 1) and upper-right corner (size, size) using nested loops ❶. We start at (1,1) so we're always calculating GCDs of pairs of positive integers. For every visible lattice point whose coordinates yield a GCD of 1, we increment the count variable.

After the loops are completed, we use the value of count to approximate π. We already know the following:

$$\frac{6}{\pi^2} \approx \frac{count}{(size)^2}$$

Solving for π, we get:

$$\pi \approx \sqrt{\frac{6(\text{size})^2}{\text{count}}}$$

We make this calculation at the end of the program ❷.

The Results

It's fun to run this program for a fairly large square, say size = 1000, and watch Scratch Cat take a few seconds to tally the points as they're counted. Figure 8-15 shows the results. As before, the larger the sample size, the more accurate the approximation is likely to be.

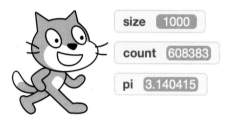

size `1000`

count `608383`

pi `3.140415`

Figure 8-15: Visible lattice points in a square of size 1,000

Once again, the value of π is accurate for at least the first few decimal places.

Programming Challenges

8.3 The series behind the visible lattice point enumeration is:

$$\pi^2/6 = 1 + 1/4 + 1/9 + 1/16 + \dots + 1/n^2 + \dots$$

Use Scratch to check this out by working out the first several partial sums:

$$1, 1 + 1/4, 1 + 1/4 + 1/9, \dots$$

8.4 A formula for π involving an infinite series is $\pi/4 = 1 - 1/3 + 1/5 - 1/7 + \dots$. This is sometimes called the *Gregory series*. Program Scratch to use this formula to get the first few digits of π.

8.5 The series in Challenge 8.3 consists of all positive terms, while the Gregory series has terms that alternate between positive and negative. Compare how many terms of each series it takes to get a value of π that's accurate to three decimal places. In general, alternating series converge much more slowly than series of positive terms.

(continued)

8.6 In Project 31, we used two versions of the area calculation to approximate π: one using every point in the square and one sampling points at random. Try applying a similar random approach to Project 32. Examine a random sampling of lattice points, count how many have relatively prime coordinates, and use that count to approximate π.

Conclusion

The number π comes up in lots of places in math, which leads to many different techniques for calculating its approximate value. Because of the limits of the IEEE 754 floating-point representation, Scratch can't express π exactly. But then again, neither can we, since the digits of π go on forever! With Scratch Cat's help, though, we can easily approximate its value in various ways, with up to 15 or 16 digits of accuracy.

What Next?

Congratulations on making it through eight chapters of Scratch-assisted math and math-assisted Scratch! Hopefully, what you've read here has inspired you to keep experimenting and learning more. This chapter offers some ideas about where to look next, whether you want to try out another programming language or you're looking for new math problems and hacks to solve them.

Learning Other Languages

I learned to program in FORTRAN and COBOL back in the early 1970s, writing my code on punched cards between the magical job control cards and waiting at the computer center for the printed output. At a meeting of the Mathematical Association of America (MAA) at Dartmouth College in 1972, I was amazed when I had the chance to try out John Kemeny's BASIC on a time-sharing printing terminal. I could never have imagined that one day there would be a language like Scratch that was accessible to everyone, with a drag-and-drop interface, integrated sound and graphics, and the ability to perform complex calculations in the blink of an eye.

The resources that the internet makes available on demand have reshaped the world. And yet, the first program I wrote in FORTRAN in 1970 (after "Hello, world!" of course) was a basis-conversion utility like the ones in Chapter 1 for converting between binary and decimal. The toolbox of computing has changed dramatically over the years, in terms of the resources available, capabilities, and ease of use, but the mathematical ideas to be explored still have the same foundations.

These days, I wouldn't recommend learning FORTRAN or COBOL, but there are other programming languages you may want to explore. In Chapter 1, we discussed how the floating-point representation of numbers in Scratch limits the range of numbers that can be studied. Other languages are designed without these limitations, or they have standard extensions available to overcome them. Two of these languages, Python and Mathematica, are readily available and likely to be of interest for people with Scratch experience. Both are bundled with the Raspberry Pi computer, along with Scratch. Mathematica is a commercial product that runs on Linux, Windows, or macOS, while Python is freely available for download from *https://www.python.org* for many operating systems.

These two languages are especially useful for exploring applications of number theory because they natively support arbitrary-precision integer arithmetic—there's no overflow and no rounding. For example, Figure 9-1 shows Mathematica's calculation for 2^{106} (flintmax squared), the same large value we wrote a Scratch program to calculate in Chapter 1.

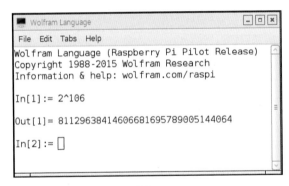

Figure 9-1: Calculating 2^{106} in Mathematica

Figure 9-2 shows the same calculation in Python.

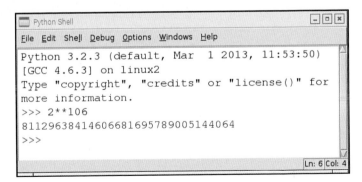

Figure 9-2: Calculating 2^{106} in Python

Not only is the calculation done with all digits reported and the answer given as a number rather than as a string, but the languages have native power operators (** or ^) that make exponential expressions easy to write without coding a loop.

Finding More Problems

If you want more math problems to explore beyond the ones in this book, the first place to look is in the world around you. You might see a list of numbers and wonder "What if...?" or notice a pattern and think "That's neat!" With Scratch, you can investigate to see what happens next. Does the pattern continue? If it does, it might be time to look for a reason. If the pattern breaks down, maybe there's a little extra side condition you can add to fix it and save the day.

There are also lots of problems that have been posed by other people that you might want to investigate. A problem posed by someone else is guaranteed to be interesting to at least one other person (the one who proposed it), and it's likely to be a Goldilocks problem: not so easy that nobody cares, and not so hard that nobody can solve it.

My all-time favorite website for problems that use computers to support mathematics is Project Euler (*https://projecteuler.net*). It offers a collection of over 800 problems to solve, with more added all the time, providing a treasure trove of computational challenges of varying types and levels of difficulty. You can track your progress and earn awards for solving certain problems, and there's a forum where you can chat with fellow solvers who share their insights and their code.

As the Project Euler site says, each problem has been designed according to a "one-minute rule." This means that although it may take several hours of thinking and coding to design a successful algorithm for solving a problem, an efficient program will allow even a modestly powered computer to produce the answer in less than a minute. For example, here's the first problem on the site:

> If we list all the natural numbers below 10 that are multiples of 3 or 5, we get 3, 5, 6, and 9. The sum of these multiples is 23.
> Find the sum of all the multiples of 3 or 5 below 1,000.

Let's take a Scratch approach to it!

Project 33: Hacking Project Euler Problem 1

Figure 9-3 shows some code that sums all the multiples of 3 or 5 up to a given limit.

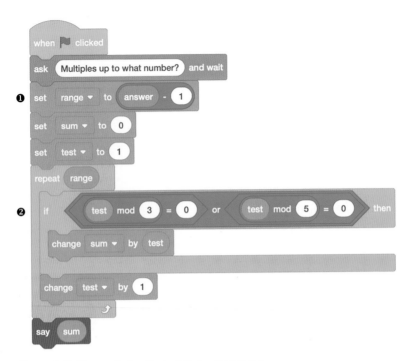

Figure 9-3: The code for Project Euler Problem 1

It's a repeat loop that tests each number from 1 up to one less than the specified upper bound (the problem description says "below 1,000," so we don't include the upper bound itself in the loop ❶). We use the mod block to check for divisibility by 3 or 5 ❷ and increase the sum if either divisibility condition holds.

The Results

Let's see what Scratch Cat has to say about the problem. Figure 9-4 shows a solution for the upper bound of 1,000.

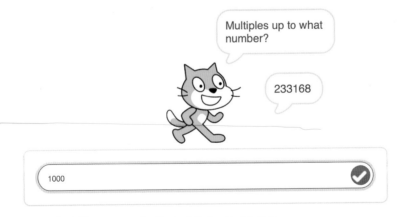

Figure 9-4: The answer to Project Euler Problem 1

It certainly takes Scratch less than a minute to generate the answer!

Hacking the Code

The Project Euler problem asked us to find the sum of all multiples of 3 and 5 below 1,000, and Scratch Cat reported an answer of 233,168. The problem description also gave 10 as an example and reported a sum of 23. What if we try other powers of 10? Table 9-1 shows some results.

Table 9-1: Sums of Multiples of 3 and 5

Upper bound	Sum
10	23
100	2,318
1,000	233,168
10,000	23,331,668
100,000	2,333,316,668
1,000,000	233,333,166,668
10,000,000	23,333,331,666,668

It looks like a pattern is emerging (look at all those repeated 3s and 6s!), but when we get to higher powers of 10 the code bogs down. The problem is that the program screens each number, so it has to count all the way up to the ending value. It takes 1 million times as long to count to 1 billion as it does to count to 1,000. That means even if your computer can count to 1,000 in 1 second, it will take 1 million seconds, or over 11 days, to count to 1 billion. Depending on how patient you are, this may be too long to wait for an answer.

Ideally, there would be a way to add up all the multiples of 3 or 5 without counting them all one at a time. The key is to see that the multiples of 3 added together are 3 + 6 + 9 + ... = 3(1 + 2 + 3 + ...) and to then recognize that 1 + 2 + 3 + ... is a sequence of triangular numbers, like the ones we discussed in Chapter 4. Likewise, the multiples of 5 added together are 5 + 10 + 15 + ... = 5(1 + 2 + 3 + ...).

We have a formula from Chapter 4 for calculating the nth triangular number, which was derived from Figure 4-13:

$$t(n) = \frac{n(n + 1)}{2}$$

We can use this formula to streamline the counting process, as shown in Figure 9-5.

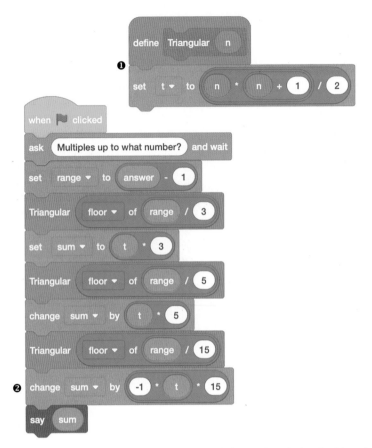

Figure 9-5: A triangular number approach for Project Euler Problem 1

First, we make a custom block to calculate the *n*th triangular number ❶. We then use this block three times in our main program. The first time, we pass in floor of range/3, then multiply the result by 3. This gives us the sum of all the multiples of 3 up to range. The second time, we pass in floor of range/5 and multiply the result by 5, which gives us the sum of all multiples of 5 up to range.

Adding these two numbers together gets us close to the answer, but there's a problem: any multiples of 15 have been counted twice, as multiples of 3 and multiples of 5. So we use the Triangular block one more time, passing in floor of range/15 and multiplying the result by 15. This gives us the sum of all the multiples of 15 up to range, which we subtract from sum to get the final result ❷. This hack is a general trick called the *principle of inclusion–exclusion*; you can use it anytime you want to keep track of how often multiple overlapping conditions are satisfied without counting the overlaps twice.

Sure enough, this code gives output matching the first version of the program, with the advantage that it gives the answer quickly all the way up to flintmax.

Programming Challenges

9.1 Change the code in Figure 9-3 to allow a different pair of multiples than 3 and 5. Have Scratch Cat ask what multiples to use and build them into your program.

9.2 Make the code in Figure 9-5 work for different pairs of multiples, too. Be careful here: you need to make sure your solution works even if the numbers aren't relatively prime.

9.3 Figure out how to program the inclusion–exclusion hack when there are three relatively prime multiples to screen rather than two.

Beyond Project Euler

If you've burned through Project Euler and you're ready for more, here are some search terms you can try out in your favorite search engine that might lead you to some other interesting problems:

Math challenge problems This will probably turn up problems with lots of different difficulty levels; choose the ones that are right for you.

Scratch challenges A lot of these focus on graphics and games, but you'll find some math challenges, too.

Scratch math games This is more likely to turn up math-focused exercises and ideas.

MAA *Convergence* This will lead you to a journal of the Mathematical Association of America, *Convergence*, that has a nice list of open access problems organized chronologically, geographically, or by subject. The emphasis isn't usually on programming, but sometimes a little bit of experimentation is a good way to understand what's going on.

There's always a chance that searches like these will turn up problems that are too easy or too hard. But even if a problem bores you or baffles you, it might be a gateway to an interesting variation that's just right.

More Scratch Projects to Explore

If you want to find more math projects specifically for Scratch, a great place to look is the Scratch website, *https://scratch.mit.edu*. There's a search box at the top (see Figure 9-6) that you can use to find all kinds of projects that members of the community have posted.

Figure 9-6: Where to look for more math in Scratch

The Scratch philosophy is that code is to be shared, and anything that's been posted on the site is available to copy and extend, as long as you give credit to the original poster. There are lots of programs that are first efforts and good for easy play, as well as some very elaborate work.

Here are some search terms for the Scratch website that will lead you to interesting projects related to the programs we've built in this book:

Chapter 1: What Computers Think About Numbers

* binary clock
* ternary
* octal
* decimal fraction
* binary search
* math parser
* floating point

Chapter 2: Exploring Divisibility and Primes

* modular times table
* twin prime
* Eratosthenes
* grid sequence
* fraction adder
* Egyptian fraction
* divisibility test

Chapter 3: Splitting Numbers with Prime Factorization

* trial division
* factorization
* Mersenne prime
* sum of divisors
* Fermat prime
* semiprime (another word for *biprime*)
* Lucas–Lehmer
* Spirograph
* repunit (a number like 1111 that contains only the digit 1)

Chapter 4: Finding Patterns in Sequences

* Fibonacci
* Padovan
* triangular number

Conclusion

Scratch is like a mental amplifier, letting you see more deeply into patterns than you could on your own. We've used Scratch in this book to explore arithmetic, number theory, geometry, cryptography, sequences, and arrays—and that's just the beginning of what it can do.

Whether you stick with Scratch or go on to other programming languages, the algorithms and the way of seeing the world with computer-aided vision that Scratch provides can help you be a more creative thinker. I hope to see you someday at my Scratch studio (*https://scratch.mit.edu/studios/29153814*), and I'd love to see any variations or extensions of this book's programs you decide to share. Until then, keep on coding!

Programming Challenge Hints

Studying math involves learning and understanding mathematical concepts in class, using textbooks and worksheets. It can be a passive process, where you just try to absorb information. On the other hand, *doing* math involves actively applying concepts to solve problems and create new mathematical models. This process requires creativity and problem-solving skills, as well as the ability to think critically and logically.

Programming is an important part of doing math, as it lets you automate complex calculations and constructions in order to explore mathematical ideas in ways that would be impossible on paper or in your head. This book has been all about using Scratch to do math—writing algorithms and performing numerical computations—with the programming challenges being an invitation for you to "get your hands dirty" on some real problems. This chapter provides some comments and code snippets to help you solve those challenges.

Chapter 1: What Computers Think About Numbers

Challenge 1.1

As a first step, you could make a list of the digits in the base *b* number with a loop like the one in Figure A-1. Then, you could put the digits together in a string to make the answer look like a base *b* number with code like that in Figure A-2.

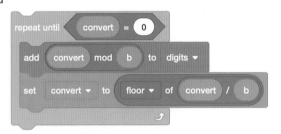

Figure A-1: Converting to base b

For base 11 or 12, check if convert mod *b* is 10 or 11 and, if so, substitute T or E before adding the result to the digits list.

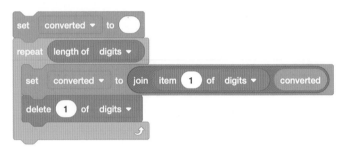

Figure A-2: Joining the digits into a string

Challenge 1.2

Figure A-3 shows some code that works for base 11 or base 12. You can add cases to it to support base 16.

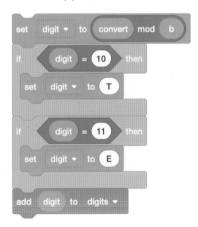

Figure A-3: Substituting letters
for numbers

When you go from binary to hexadecimal, each group of four binary digits (counting from the least significant, or rightmost, digit) is equivalent to a single hexadecimal digit. For example, 1011 in binary becomes E in hexadecimal.

Challenge 1.3

You can grow a list by adding new items to it. Suppose you've asked the user to specify a starting value for the list, what the change should be (stored in the variable change), and how long the list should be (stored in the variable length). Figure A-4 shows some code to calculate the remaining values in the list based on exponential and linear growth. Each type of growth gets its own list.

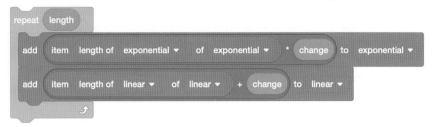

Figure A-4: Comparing exponential and linear growth

Challenge 1.4

With linear growth it would take a hopelessly long time to count to Scratch's absolute maximum number, but with exponential growth (see Challenge 1.3) you can get there very quickly. By doubling, for example, it takes just 1,024 steps. The largest number Scratch can represent is about $1.08 \cdot 10^{308}$; beyond that, the value reported is Infinity. Figure A-5 shows how to get there.

Challenge 1.5

The best way to approach this challenge is to treat the 64 binary digits in the IEEE representation as a string. Luckily, there's room on the Scratch stage to show the complete value of a variable holding 64 characters. Figure A-6 numbers the characters (grouped by tens) to demonstrate how wide the screen is, though you'll want use just the characters 0 and 1 for the actual binary representation.

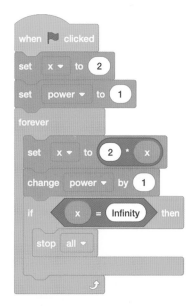

Figure A-5: Doubling your way to infinity

x `12345678901234567890123456789012345678901234567890123456789012345678901234`

letter 64 of x

4

Figure A-6: There's room on the stage for 64 bits.

Treating the binary representation as a string lets you pick out individual bits with the letter of block. You might want to store the bits in a list to make it easier to manipulate them.

Challenge 1.6

To calculate 3^n, all you need to do is change the multiplier from 2 to 3 in the replace item block ❶ in Figure 1-13. Figure A-7 shows the updated block.

Figure A-7: Calculating powers of 3 rather than powers of 2

Challenge 1.7

Make sure that when you translate the answer back from a list of five-digit blocks to a string, smaller numbers are padded with an appropriate number of zeros. If the "digit" is 435, for example, it should become 00435 before being joined to the string. You can do this with a few if blocks.

Challenge 1.8

Start by prompting for a number. Treat it as a string and make a list of digits by taking the characters from the string one at a time, beginning with the rightmost character (the least significant digit). Make a similar list from the second number. Add the corresponding digits in the two lists and keep the carry separate, if one occurs, so you can add it to the next pair of digits. If the numbers have a different amount of digits, you can pad the smaller number with 0 entries in its list of digits to finish the addition.

Chapter 2: Exploring Divisibility and Primes

Challenge 2.1

Figure A-8 shows a custom block that can be used in an infinite loop both for Scratch Cat's turn and for screening your answer to see if you have the pattern correct. It checks if a number is divisible by 5, 7, or 35 (both 5 and 7) and "translates" the number to the appropriate phrase.

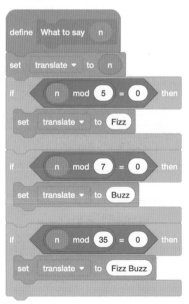

Figure A-8: A block to play Fizz-Buzz

Challenge 2.2

To calculate the alternating digit sum, it helps to view the input number n as a string, like we do in the casting out nines program from Figure 2-2. Then, the digits of n can be treated as characters and pulled out for individual treatment as letter i of n. To alternate between addition and subtraction, make a variable called plus minus and toggle it back and forth between 1 and -1 by multiplying it by -1 after each digit. Figure A-9 has some code to get you started.

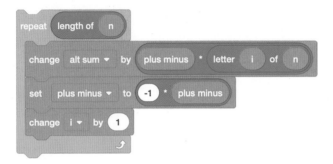

Figure A-9: Testing for divisibility by 11 using an alternating digit sum

Challenge 2.3

The code in Figure A-10 counts how many random numbers are divisible by 9.

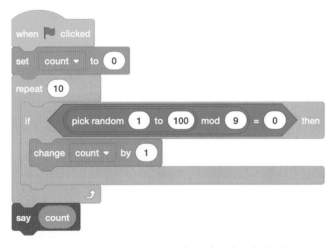

Figure A-10: Testing random numbers for divisibility by 9

This is a bit of a trick problem, though. You would think that about 1/9 of the numbers would be divisible by 9, but in the particular range from 1 to 100 there are 100 numbers and only 11 multiples of 9, so the actual probability is 11/100, which is a little smaller than 1/9. Still, with such a small sample size it would be hard to spot the difference.

Challenge 2.4

At the end of the casting out nines program, the variable x holds the "check digit." It's easy to add that digit to the original number if you treat the numbers as strings and use a join block, as in Figure A-11.

Figure A-11: Adding a "check digit" to a number

Scratch Cat doesn't have to say the answer with the check digit. You can just leave the variable with check digit visible on the stage.

Challenge 2.5

Casting out nines won't help catch an error of transposition, since the sum of the digits is the same no matter what order the digits are in.

Challenge 2.6

Table A-1 shows how the ratio of primes evolves as the upper bound increases.

Table A-1: The Ratio of Primes

Upper bound	Prime count	Ratio
10	4	0.4
100	25	0.25
1,000	168	0.168
10,000	1,229	0.1229
100,000	9,592	0.09592

The relative number of primes appears to decrease.

Challenge 2.7

You're looking for consecutive runs of false in the sieve output. There are 77 in a row starting at 188,030.

Challenge 2.8

Figure A-12 shows a snippet of code to add to scan the `primes` list for twin primes.

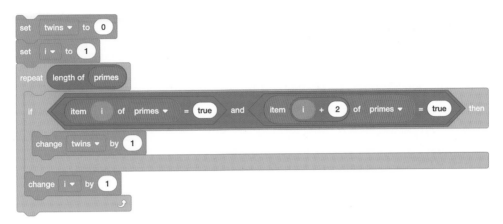

Figure A-12: Looking for twin primes

Challenge 2.9

The easiest way to do this is probably to make a new list where each entry contains six consecutive numbers from the original `primes` list joined together in a string. When you view the resulting list on the Scratch stage, it will look like a table with six columns. You'll have to be careful with the formatting, though, so that numbers of different lengths in each column line up nicely. (See Project 21 in Chapter 5 for an example of how to achieve this sort of formatting.)

Column 2 consists of all numbers that are congruent to 2 mod 6, which are divisible by 2. The elements in columns 4 and 6 are also all divisible by 2, and the elements in column 3 are divisible by 3. This means the only places primes could be after the first row are in columns 1 and 5.

Challenge 2.10

As discussed in "Hacking the Code" on page 39 (Project 9), you can keep track of runtimes using the `timer` block in the Sensing section of Scratch's block menu. Set a variable called `timer1` when you start a calculation and one called `timer2` when you're done, and calculate the difference (`timer2 - timer1`) to see how much time has elapsed, in seconds.

If you're trying to time something that happens really quickly, it might be hard to tell how much time the computer is spending working on your problem and how much time it's spending on its own background tasks. To get a better estimate, you could have the computer repeat your problem a bunch of times—say, 100—and then divide the total elapsed time by that number to find the average time per run.

Challenge 2.11

You can add a step counter to the custom `gcd` block from Figure 2-17 to see how many cycles the algorithm takes. Figure A-13 shows the updated block definition.

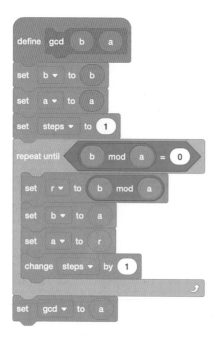

Figure A-13: Counting the steps to
complete Euclid's algorithm

The algorithm takes longer when the quotients are smaller, so keep them at 1 to make a pretty pattern of values for remainders. Work backward from 3 = 1 · 2 + 1 to 5 = 1 · 3 + 2, 8 = 1 · 5 + 3, and so on. You'll see this pattern again in Chapter 4!

Chapter 3: Splitting Numbers with Prime Factorization

Challenge 3.1

To find a perfect number, simply check if the result of the sum of divisors code (Project 12, Figure 3-8) is equal to the original input number. It turns out any even perfect number n satisfies the following equation, where $2^p - 1$ is a prime number:

$$n = 2^{p-1}(2^p - 1)$$

When $p = 2$, the equation gives the perfect number 6. When $p = 3$, it gives 28. When $p = 5$, it gives 496, and when $p = 7$, it gives 8,128.

Nobody knows if there are any odd perfect numbers.

Challenge 3.2

Figure A-14 shows some code to identify if a number is perfect, abundant, or deficient. Add it to the end of the sum of divisors program in Figure 3-8. Notice that since the sum of divisors includes the original number, answer, we first subtract answer to keep track of the sum of proper divisors ❶.

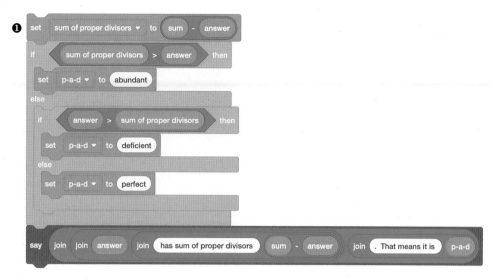

Figure A-14: Determining if a number is perfect, abundant, or deficient

Now you need to write a counting routine that loops up to some upper bound, automatically inputting numbers into the sum of divisors program. Use three variables to keep track of the number of abundant, perfect, and deficient numbers, incrementing the appropriate variable whenever each type of number is found. There are no abundant numbers up to 10, but there are 22 of them up to 100 and 246 of them up to 1,000. There are 9 deficient numbers up to 10 and 751 of them up to 1,000.

Challenge 3.3

The code gives the correct answer for a 0 exponent, even when the base is 0.

Challenge 3.4

Figure A-15 shows a modification of Figure 3-7 that allows for positive or negative exponents.

Challenge 3.5

Figure A-16 shows how you might preserve the list of exponents when you want to calculate $\tau(n)$. This code replaces the original repeat loop from the Project 11 code (see Figure 3-6).

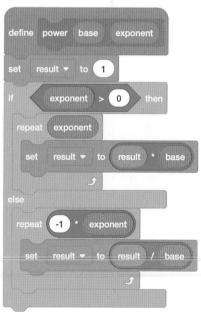

Figure A-15: Working with positive or negative exponents

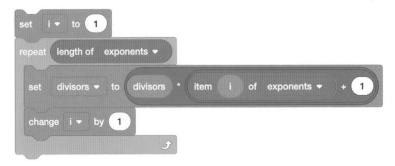

Figure A-16: Preserving the exponents list

You can use the same index variable, i, to step through both the prime factors and the exponents when calculating $\sigma(n)$.

Challenge 3.6

The custom block in Figure A-17 uses a Boolean variable, primeQ, to keep track of its answer. We start by setting primeQ to true and loop to change its value to false if p can be divided evenly by any number. We have to look only for divisors up to the square root of p.

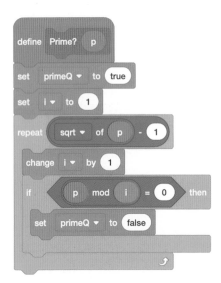

Figure A-17: Testing if a number is prime

You can make the code in Figure A-17 run more quickly by exiting after the first false.

Challenge 3.7

Figure A-18 shows a block that finds the next prime number after n.

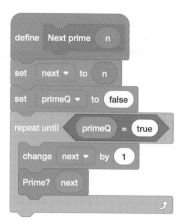

Figure A-18: Finding the next prime number

The block steps forward from n, passing values into the prime checking block from Challenge 3.6, until it reaches a number where primeQ is true.

Challenge 3.8

Think about the track the inner wheel follows as a straight line instead of the inside of a ring. For each complete rotation, the ring adds 96 teeth to the straight line track. There are LCM(b, 96) teeth in the shortest track common to 96 teeth and b teeth—that's when the wheel will end up back where it started and the drawing will be complete. A point is determined every b teeth, so there will be LCM(b, 96) / b points in all.

Challenge 3.9

You can complete this challenge with the custom block from Challenge 3.6.

Challenge 3.10

To compare the factorization methods, you can use the timer hack from Figure 2-19. The trial division method is usually quicker for numbers below flintmax, but if the number n being factored is a biprime with both prime factors close to $\sqrt{n}$, then Fermat factorization can be faster.

Challenge 3.11

Here's some general code that uses the Pen extension to paint the stage with pixels whose color values (0 for white and 1 for black) are derived from a binary message. We'll start with the initial setup block in Figure A-19.

Figure A-19: Getting ready to draw a message

This block first sets the starting coordinates to a position near the upper-left corner of the stage ❶. It then asks for a width and height, which are the numbers of columns and rows you want your message to contain. Next, it determines the size of each block in the message by dividing the stage's overall width and height by the width and height of the message. The sprite that will draw the message by adding stamps in the appropriate pixel locations is a 9×9 black square, which is scaled to fit in the grid being drawn ❷.

The code in Figure A-20 does the work of drawing the message.

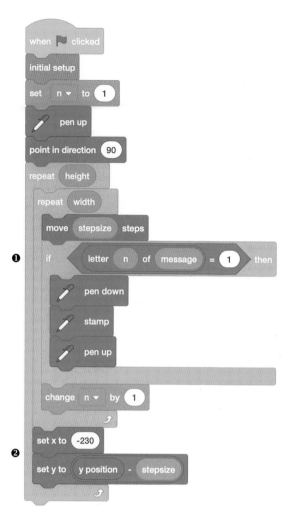

```
when ⚑ clicked
initial setup
set  n ▾  to  1
🖋 pen up
point in direction  90
repeat  height
  repeat  width
    move  stepsize  steps
❶ if  ⟨ letter  n  of  message  =  1 ⟩ then
      🖋 pen down
      🖋 stamp
      🖋 pen up

    change  n ▾  by  1

  set x to  -230
❷ set y to  y position  -  stepsize
```

Figure A-20: Drawing the message

We specify the size of the rectangle for the message in two loops, one for the height and one for the width. The message is a string of bits (0s and 1s). We use the variable n to look at the message bit by bit, drawing a stamp for each bit that's a 1 ❶. At the end of each row, we move the cursor to the start of the next row ❷.

You can use this program to draw the contents of the Arecibo message by copying and pasting in its 1,679 bits, or entering them by hand if you want to. Or you can test the program on the smaller message included in the sample message variable used in the "3-PC11 Binary message to pixels" Scratch project created by rumpus88366 (*https://scratch.mit.edu/projects/771257850*), shown in Figure A-21.

```
set  sample message ▾  to  0011110001000001110000001000111100
```

Figure A-21: A test message

This message gives a much simpler output when drawn as a rectangle seven columns wide by five rows high (see Figure A-22). Let's call it an *S* for *Scratch*!

Figure A-22: Visualizing
the test message

You could extend this program in various ways. For example, the program could just ask for the message and factor the message's length to find appropriate dimensions for the rectangle, assuming the length is a biprime.

Chapter 4: Finding Patterns in Sequences

Challenge 4.1

The Lucas sequence begins 2, 1, 3, 4, 7, 11, 18, 29, 47,.... There are lots of interesting relationships between Lucas numbers (represented with an *l*) and Fibonacci numbers (represented with an *f*). For example:

$$f_{n-2} + f_n = l_n$$

Challenge 4.2

To extend the Fibonacci numbers backward from f_1, we need to make sense of f_0, f_{-1}, f_{-2}, and so on. We can start by saying f_0 should be whatever we need to add to $f_1 = 1$ to get $f_2 = 1$. Therefore, $f_0 = 0$. To maintain the recurrence, we need $f_{-1} = 1$, $f_{-2} = -1$, $f_{-3} = 2$, and so on. It's the original Fibonacci sequence, but every other value is negative.

The program in Figure A-23 uses a series of if statements to report the Fibonacci number with a given index, negative indices included.

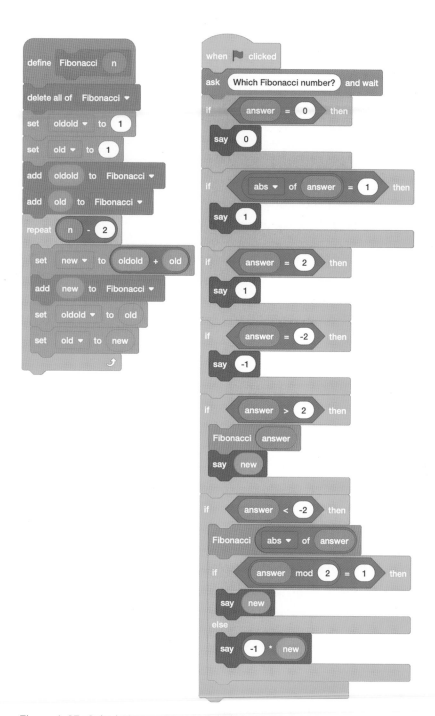

Figure A-23: Calculating positive and negative Fibonacci terms

The first few if statements account for the initial values of the sequence, between indices –2 and +2. For other indices, the custom Fibonacci block calculates the Fibonacci number as if the index were positive. For odd negative indices, the result is switched to a negative number.

Challenge 4.3

The last value before flintmax is at row 78. The last value before the result is reported as Infinity is at row 1,476.

Challenge 4.4

To generate the coefficients, you need to know the values of terms 0, 1, and 2 in the sequence. Let's call these values r, s, and t, respectively. (In Chapter 4, we mostly talked about sequences as starting with term 1, but they can also have a term 0.) We can think of these three values as the results of the quadratic polynomial function $f(x) = ax^2 + bx + c$ when x equals 0, 1, and 2.

Think about what happens to the quadratic polynomial when x is 0:

$$f(x) = ax^2 + bx + c$$
$$f(0) = (a \cdot 0^2) + (b \cdot 0) + c$$
$$= 0 + 0 + c$$
$$= c$$

The coefficients a and b go away, leaving only c. So what we're calling r, the value of term 0 in the sequence, must also be the value of c. What about the case where $x = 1$?

$$f(1) = (a \cdot 1^2) + (b \cdot 1) + c$$
$$= a + b + c$$

This tells us that term 1 in the sequence, what we're calling s, is the sum of the three coefficients. And what about when $x = 2$?

$$f(2) = (a \cdot 2^2) + (b \cdot 2) + c$$
$$= 4a + 2b + c$$

This is equivalent to term 2 in the sequence, what we're calling t.

With a little algebra, we can use these results to write individual formulas for a, b, and c. They are:

$$a = \frac{t - 2s + r}{2} \qquad b = 2s - \frac{t}{2} - \frac{3r}{2} \qquad c = r$$

In your program, you'll take terms 0, 1, and 2 from a sequence and plug them into these formulas as the variables r, s, and t. For the sequence of pentagonal numbers, you should get $a = 3/2$, $b = -1/2$, and $c = 0$.

This neat math hack for figuring out the coefficients from the first few values of the quadratic polynomial is called the *method of undetermined coefficients*.

Challenge 4.5

This is a sneaky way of asking for the longest set of consecutive composite numbers you can find. You solved that problem in Challenge 2.7.

Challenge 4.6

Figure A-24 modifies the decimal-to-binary converter from Project 1 to generate a list of binary numbers. The new How many ones? block counts the number of 1s in each binary number and stores the results in a separate list to create the desired sequence.

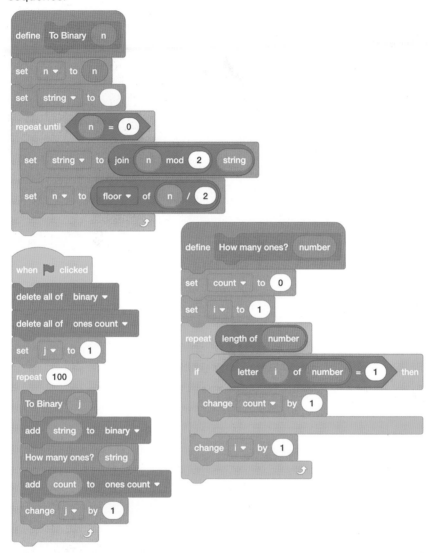

Figure A-24: Counting the 1s in binary numbers

One way to think about the sequence is to see it as blocks of 1, 2, 4, 8,..., elements. (The length of each block is a power of 2.) To get the next block, first copy the previous block, then follow this with a second copy of the previous block but with 1 added to each element. For example:

* The first block is 1.
* The second block is 1, 1 + 1 (or 1, 2).
* The third block is 1, 2, 1 + 1, 2 + 1 (or 1, 2, 2, 3).
* The fourth block is 1, 2, 2, 3, 1 + 1, 2 + 1, 2 + 1, 3 + 1 (or 1, 2, 2, 3, 2, 3, 3, 4).

An interesting feature of this sequence is the way it contains copies of itself. If you look at just the elements in positions 2, 4, 6, 8, 10, ..., you'll see that they're exactly the same as the original sequence!

Challenge 4.7

The Fibonacci numbers show up again in the first, second, and higher differences.

Challenge 4.8

Similar to the Fibonacci numbers, the powers of 2 show up again in the first, second, and higher differences. It's the underlying exponential growth of both sequences that makes their differences show the same pattern.

Challenge 4.9

Third differences are constant, and fourth and higher differences are 0. It's significant that for the sequence of squares, the second differences are constant with a value of $2 \cdot 1 = 2$, whereas for cubes, the third differences are constant with a value of $3 \cdot 2 \cdot 1 = 6$. One more pattern to check out!

Chapter 5: From Sequences to Arrays

Challenge 5.1

There's a zero at the end of $n!$ for every factor of 10. A factor of 10 comes from a factor of 5 and a factor of 2. There are lots of factors of 2, so it's easier to count factors of 5. Every fifth number is a multiple of 5 and contributes a factor of 5 to $n!$ There are floor of n/5 multiples of 5 up to n. In addition, there are extra factors of 5 that come from higher powers of 5. For example, every 25th number is a multiple of 25, which contributes an extra factor of 5, and every 125th number is a multiple of 125, contributing yet another extra factor of 5. The program in Figure A-25 counts just the factors of 5 the first time through the repeat until loop, then uses additional cycles of the loop to count the extra factors that come from factors of higher powers of 5.

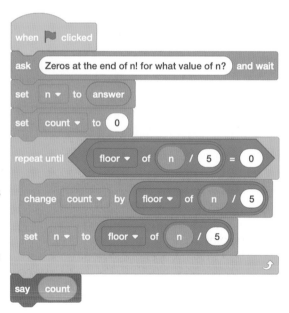

Figure A-25: Calculating the number of zeros at the end of n factorial

The program reports that there are six zeros at the end of 25 factorial.

Challenge 5.2

You can adapt the row-generating program from Project 19 (Figure 5-7) to grab row entries after the row is calculated. Figure A-26 shows a custom block to calculate the row and extract the *k*th entry. You could also do the calculation as a quotient of factorials, as we did in Project 18 (Figure 5-1), but this way gives answers that are accurate for more rows.

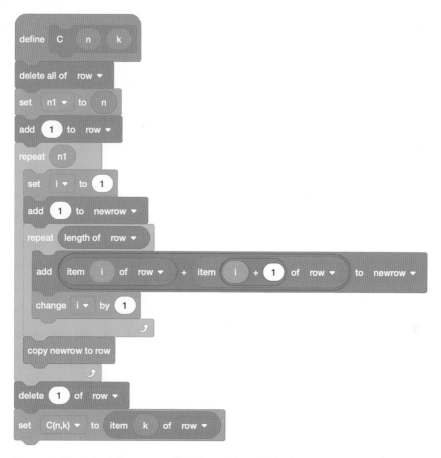

Figure A-26: Calculating a specific binomial coefficient

You'll want to call this custom block repeatedly for successive values of n while holding k constant at 2, adding each set of results to its own list. You should find that the numbers down the C(*n*, 2) diagonal are the triangular numbers.

Challenge 5.3

The trick is to take mod 2 of each value, so even numbers end up as 0s and odd numbers end up as 1s. Figure A-27 shows an interpretation of the first 32 rows of Pascal's triangle, mod 2. Here, the 1s are visualized as black squares and the 0s as blank spaces.

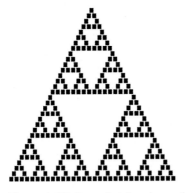

Figure A-27: Pascal's triangle mod 2

The resulting pattern is known as the Sierpiński triangle. It's a famous example of a *fractal*, a pattern that repeats itself at different scales.

Challenge 5.4

You can use the custom gcd block from Project 9 (see Figure 2-17) to filter the row and column indices, then include in the table only entries where the row and column indices are both relatively prime to the modulus. Figure A-28 shows the updates to the code.

Figure A-28: Restricting the operations table to rows and columns that are relatively prime to the modulus

The stack on the left goes in the definition for the Make index row block (see Figure 5-15), taking the place of the set row block inside the repeat modulus loop.

The stack on the right goes into the main program stack (see Figure 5-17), replacing the current add row to table block.

With these changes, the mod 12 multiplication table comes out looking like Figure A-29.

Challenge 5.5

You can modify the custom power block from Project 12 (see Figure 3-7) to work with modular arithmetic so it takes in a base and a power and calculates the appropriate power of the base, mod p. Then, you can build a custom

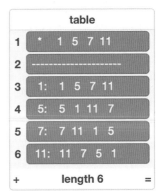

Figure A-29: A reduced multiplication table mod 12

Boolean block to test if a particular number n is a primitive root of a particular prime p. Figure A-30 shows these two blocks.

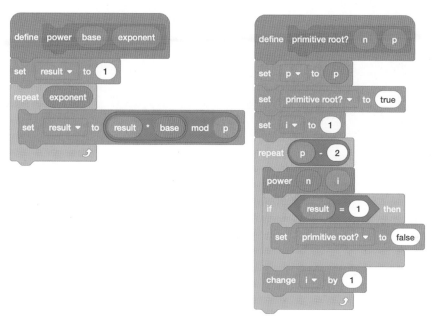

Figure A-30: Looking for a primitive root

The loop in the primitive root? block goes to p - 2 because if you haven't found a power of n that equals 1 by this time, the last power will be 1, and n will be a primitive root.

With those pieces, the main program is just a loop to ask for a prime and find the first number that works as a primitive root. Two math questions to consider as a follow-up are why primes must have primitive roots and whether primitive roots exist for any composite numbers.

Challenge 5.6

You can strip down the Make index row block from Figure 5-15 to eliminate the work of formatting the table with an index row and padding appropriately with spaces. Then, modify the custom pad block in Figure 5-16 to insert a comma before x instead of one or more spaces.

You might also want to strip off the initial comma at the start of each row before adding it to the table. You can do that with another custom block. Scratch doesn't have a command to identify and modify characters in strings the way it lets us work with elements of lists, so you can just rewrite the string from the second character on, as shown in Figure A-31.

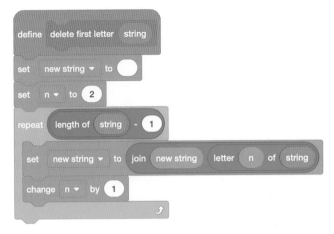

Figure A-31: Removing the first character from a string

Chapter 6: Making Codes, and Cracking Them Too

Challenge 6.1

Make a single ring of letters in your favorite drawing program, similar to Figure A-32. Import it into Scratch as a sprite labeled Outer Wheel.

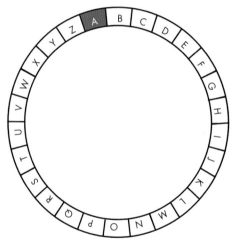

Figure A-32: A letter ring

Now shrink the Outer Wheel sprite to make a new sprite that's small enough to fit inside it, and label this Inner Wheel. The only code you need is a bit of code to manipulate the smaller sprite, as shown in Figure A-33.

Figure A-33: Rotating Inner Wheel one letter at a time

This code rotates the inner wheel to the left or right. The angle of 13.846 degrees is 360 / 26, so each key press shifts the inner wheel by one letter at a time relative to the outer wheel.

Challenge 6.2

H becomes I, A becomes B, and L becomes M (see Figure A-34).

Figure A-34: Shifting "HAL" by 1

Challenge 6.3

Yes in French is *oui*. Your decoder ring can translate this word for you using a shift of 16: Y becomes O, E becomes U, and S becomes I (see Figure A-35). Sadly, its magical translation capabilities don't extend much further!

Figure A-35: YES?

Challenge 6.4

This is a job for the program from Project 23 (see Figure 6-9). A shift of 16 reveals the message "THERE WILL BE A HOT TIME IN THE OLD TOWN TONIGHT!"

Challenge 6.5

The trouble here is that, due to the order of operations, the multiplication happens before the shift when you run the linear transformation code. If you try to undo both at once, the multiplier acts on the shift as well, so the shift ends up being incorrect. This is why we originally performed the decryption in two steps, to force the shift to be reversed before the multiplication.

If *s* is the original shift factor, the fix is to take –*s* and multiply it by the modular inverse (mod the alphabet size). Then, use the result as the new shift factor for the decryption, while using the modular inverse as the new multiplier. This way, when the multiplier is applied, the inverse cancels out and you get the shift you want.

Challenge 6.6

The program in Figure A-36 achieves this. After prompting for a modulus, which is the alphabet size, and a multiplier, it calls our custom gcd block (from Figure 2-17) to make sure a modular inverse exists. The program exits if no inverse exists, and otherwise it calculates the inverse by trial and error ❶. Then, it prompts for the shift and calculates the inverse transformation's shift ❷.

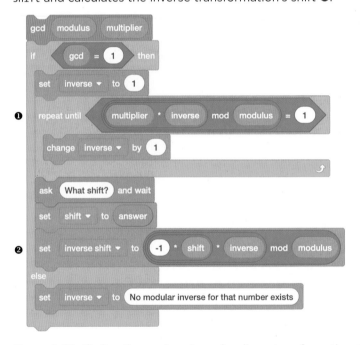

Figure A-36: Finding the numbers to undo a linear transformation cipher

Challenge 6.7

If the multiplier isn't relatively prime to the alphabet size, the scrambled alphabet won't be complete. Some letters will occur more than once, and others won't appear at all. Also, there's no modular inverse, so no decryption is possible.

Challenge 6.8

You can reuse some of the code we wrote earlier in the chapter for this challenge, including the Alphabet block from Figure 6-2 to build the alphabet list and the Scramble block from Figure 6-19 to mix up the alphabet. You'll also need an Initialize block to set up the alphabet list and prompt for a message (you won't need it to prompt for a shift and a multiplier, since you're going to generate all possible shifts and multipliers yourself), as well as our old friend the gcd block from Project 9 (Figure 2-17). Figure A-37 shows the new code.

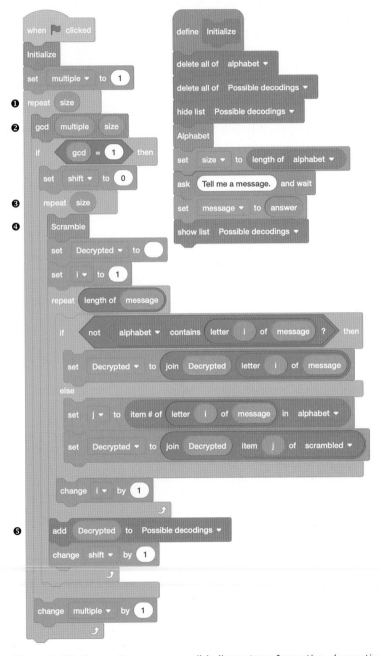

Figure A-37: Generating every possible linear transformation decryption

The outer repeat loop moves through every possible multiplier ❶, while the inner repeat loop moves through every possible shift for that multiplier ❸. Together, these loops generate every possible linear transformation, using Scramble to mix up the alphabet based on the current multiple and shift parameters ❹. Each possible message is built up character by character in the encrypted variable, then added to the list of possible decodings ❺. Before exploring a given multiplier, the gcd test ❷ confirms that the multiplier and the alphabet size are relatively prime. This indicates that a modular inverse exists for the multiplier and therefore that the multiplier is valid.

Challenge 6.9

An easy way to mix up the alphabet is to swap each letter with a random letter. Figure A-38 shows a program that does this using a custom swap block. Notice that you need an extra variable, x, to temporarily hold one of the swapped values.

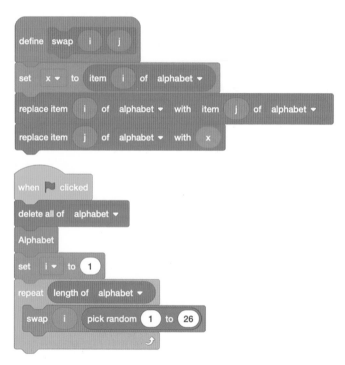

Figure A-38: Randomly scrambling the alphabet

If you'd like to see the entire scrambled alphabet on the stage, you can build a string from the alphabet list, adding one character at a time (see Figure A-39).

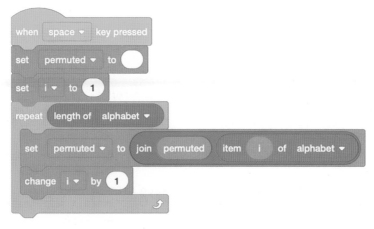

Figure A-39: Viewing the scrambled alphabet as a single string

Challenge 6.10

Start with an extension of the gcd code, shown in Figure A-40, that remembers the quotients and remainders as qlist and rlist.

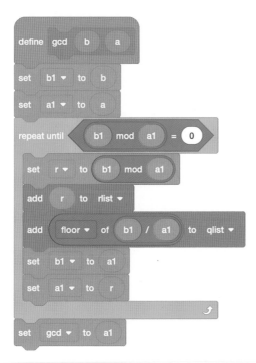

Figure A-40: Listing quotients and remainders
from Euclid's algorithm

You can now make linear combinations of the remainders to represent the greatest common divisor. As you substitute up from the bottom, you end up with a linear combination of the original numbers a and b that gives the GCD. Figure A-41 shows how this works.

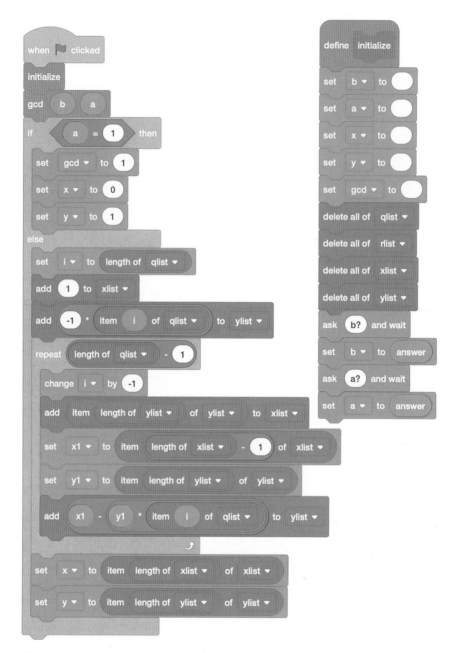

Figure A-41: Finding x and y

As an example, if you ask the program to use *b* = 26 and *a* = 17, you'll end up with x = 2 and y = -3. That means (2 · 26) – (3 · 17) = 1, which tells you that –3 · 17 ≡ 1 mod 26. So you can use –3, or 26 – 3 = 23, as the modular inverse for 17. Figure A-42 shows the output for this scenario.

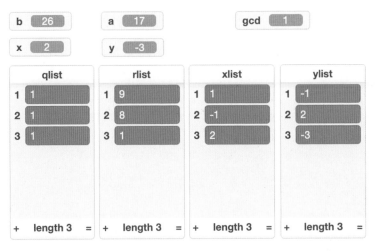

Figure A-42: Identifying –3 (or +23) as the modular inverse of 17

Challenge 6.11

The logic of this program is in its main part, shown in Figure A-43.

Figure A-43: Guessing a letter and seeing how it fits

The custom Initialize block asks for a cryptogram to solve and sets up the stage display, showing the puzzle and the shape of its solution. Then, the forever loop asks for a letter in the puzzle to guess and what it should be replaced with. It's easier to process the guess if the solution is maintained as a list of individual characters rather than as a string, so there's some background coding to convert back and forth between Solution, which is displayed, and Solution list, which remains hidden. The bookkeeping is done in the update block, shown in Figure A-44.

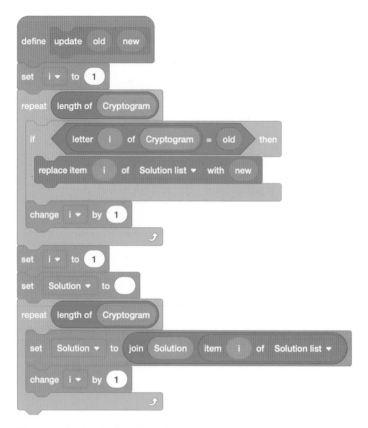

Figure A-44: Updating the solution

Challenge 6.12

Figure A-45 shows a quick way to tell whether a character is a letter or not. The Boolean variable letterQ is set to true for upper- or lowercase letters, or false otherwise. (The contains block doesn't care about capitalization.)

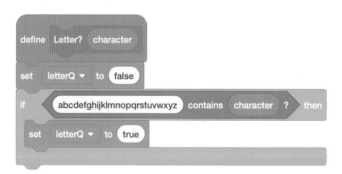

Figure A-45: Testing for letters of the alphabet

Once you have this block, you can use it to test each character in a string, one at a time. Keep only those characters that result in a letterQ value of true.

Chapter 7: Experiments in Counting

Challenge 7.1

The program in Figure A-46 lists Catalan numbers using the alternative recurrence.

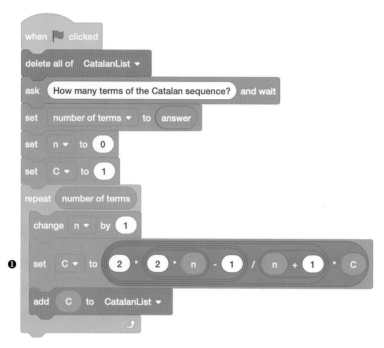

Figure A-46: Another Catalan recurrence

The calculation is implemented inside the repeat loop ❶. Notice that the formula is a single-term recurrence, meaning we need only $C(n - 1)$ to calculate C. This means we can just use the C variable over and over, without having to look up earlier values in the list. Also, term $C(0)$ doesn't have to be included in the list at all, so the list's index numbers are correct from the start. This recurrence produces accurate values up to flintmax.

Challenge 7.2

The input for this program will be a row of the Catalan list generated by the code for Project 28 (Figures 7-1 through 7-3), consisting of forward slash (/) and backslash (\) characters. Say you've extracted one of the rows into the input pattern variable. You can then draw the pattern with the code in Figure A-47.

Figure A-47: Visualizing Catalan paths

The custom draw block sets step size to make the drawing fit nicely on the stage. Then, the repeat loop in the main stack uses the characters as a recipe for drawing the diagram, ignoring all characters in input pattern except for the slashes. It draws a diagonal line upward for each forward slash and a diagonal line downward for each backslash.

Challenge 7.3

The pattern to notice is that the *n*th Catalan number is $C(2n, n) / (n + 1)$.

Challenge 7.4

All you have to do is change every / to a left parenthesis and every \ to a right parenthesis. To label the parentheses with letters (placing the label after a left parenthesis and before a right parenthesis) so it looks like a multiplication problem, it might be easiest to do two passes through each string in the Catalan list. The first pass can change each slash to the appropriate parenthesis and add a placeholder symbol for a letter (the code in Figure A-48 uses a + symbol). The second pass can then replace each placeholder with the next unused letter in the alphabet.

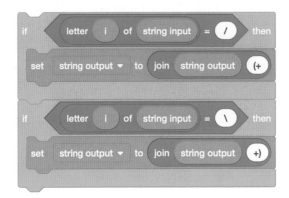

Figure A-48: Representing Catalan numbers with parentheses

Figure A-49 shows what the output would look like for a given input string.

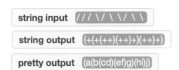

Figure A-49: The pretty output variable substitutes letters for plus signs.

Challenges 7.5 and 7.6

Let's assume that a partition is presented as a string of summands connected by + signs, as we saw in the list shown in Figure 7-15. We'll also assume the summands are in increasing order. Since you need to look at each summand, the first step could be to change the string into a list of individual summands called parts. Then, you can define custom blocks to report Boolean values if the list has no even elements (say, oddparts()) and if the list has no duplicated elements (say, distinctparts()). The output might look like Figure A-50.

Figure A-50: Testing for all odd and all distinct summands

An interesting observation made by mathematician Leonhard Euler, the name-sake of Project Euler, is that the number of partitions of *n* with only odd summands is the same as the number of partitions of *n* with all distinct summands.

Challenge 7.7

Ramanujan made two other observations that are relevant here: the number of partitions of any number that is 5 more than a multiple of 7 is itself divisible by 7, and the number of partitions of any number that is 6 more than a multiple of 11 is itself divisible by 11. For example, $P(19) = P(2 \cdot 7 + 5) = 490$, a multiple of 7, and $P(17) = P(1 \cdot 11 + 6) = 297$, a multiple of 11.

Chapter 8: Three Helpings of Pi

Challenge 8.1

The length of the perimeter of the inscribed triangle is equal to $3\sqrt{3}$, so we should take *b*, the lower bound, to be $3\sqrt{3} / 2$. The length of the perimeter of the circumscribed triangle is equal to $6\sqrt{3}$, so *a* should be half of that, or $3\sqrt{3}$. Figure A-51 shows these new starting values.

Figure A-51: Starting values for the inscribed and circumscribed triangles

As Figure A-52 shows, running the program with these starting values does indeed produce the same results, from the second line on, as running it with starting values from hexagons.

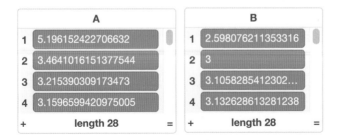

Figure A-52: The first few rows of output, starting from triangles

Challenge 8.2

All you need to do to choose random non-integer coordinates is change the two set blocks ❷ in Figure 8-11. The updated blocks are shown in Figure A-53.

Figure A-53: Randomly choosing non-integer coordinates

Not only does the code still work with non-integers, but it also gives much better approximations of π.

Challenge 8.3

Figure A-54 shows a loop to calculate a partial sum for the series up to a given number of terms.

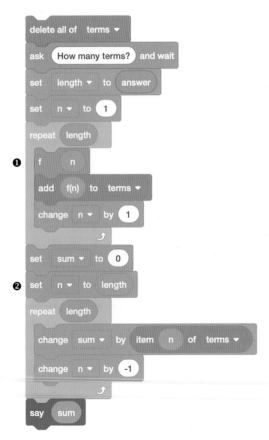

Figure A-54: Calculating partial sums for $\pi^2/6$

There are two hacks to notice here. First, we're using a custom block to calculate the nth term of the series ❶. That makes it easy to adapt the code to study other series. In this case, the custom block calculates $1/n^2$, as shown in Figure A-55.

Figure A-55: Calculating one term
of the sum

The second hack is that once we've generated a list of n terms in the series, we find their sum by adding backward from the last term to the first ❷. This is necessary because the series consists of decreasing terms, and some of the decimal places of the later terms might be wiped out if they were added to the sum of the prior (larger) terms.

If you run this program for increasingly more terms, you'll approach the value of $\pi^2/6$, which is approximately 1.644934.

Challenge 8.4

You can reuse the code from Challenge 8.3 that sums the first n terms in a series to solve this problem. You just need to define a different custom block for calculating each term, as shown in Figure A-56.

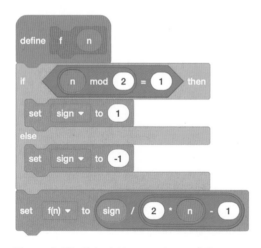

Figure A-56: Calculating one term of the sum
for $\pi/4$

This time, the terms being added are odd integers, not squares, and the signs alternate from one term to the next. So you need to introduce a new variable, sign, that switches back and forth between 1 and -1 for each term.

The value to aim for is about 0.785398, but alternating series are notoriously slow to converge, so it might take a while to get there. Multiplying this value by 4 gives an approximation of π.

Challenge 8.5

The series in Challenge 8.3 consistently reports the first three digits of π correctly after 202 terms. For the alternating series in Challenge 8.4, it takes 626 terms before the first three digits are stable.

Challenge 8.6

Unlike in the random sampling code for Project 31, you don't have the option of using non-integer coordinates (see Challenge 8.2) here because you need integers to calculate a GCD. You can still use the pick random block to generate random lattice points, though. The code in Figure A-57 has a loop using random choices of lattice point coordinates.

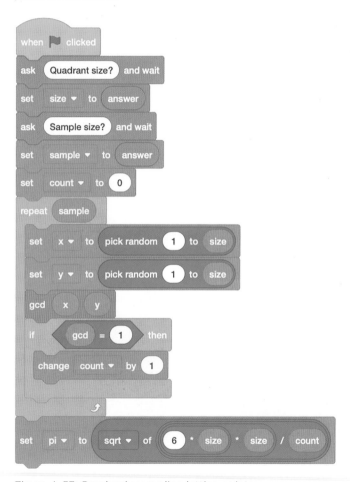

Figure A-57: Randomly sampling lattice points

It gives approximations for π that are about as good as the exhaustive enumeration using the code in Figure 8-13.

Chapter 9: What Next?

Challenge 9.1

Figure A-58 shows a program that finds the sum of the multiples of any two numbers up to a limit.

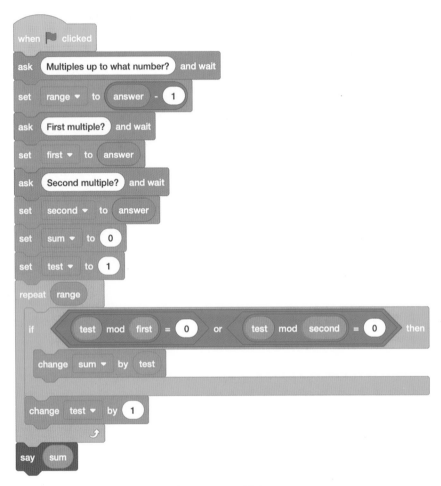

Figure A-58: Finding the sum of any two multiples

Instead of hardcoding the values of 3 and 5 into the program, as we did in Project 33, here we take in two values from the user and reference them as the first and second variables.

Challenge 9.2

You might think you can just multiply the two numbers together to get the correction, but that won't work if the numbers aren't relatively prime. Instead, you need to find the least common multiple (LCM) of the two numbers (which for relative primes happens to be the equivalent of their product). Calculating the LCM is easy using our gcd code from Project 9 (Figure 2-17), since the LCM of *b* and *a* is the product of *b* and *a* divided by their GCD, as we noted in Chapter 3.

Figure A-59 shows an updated program that sums the multiples of any two numbers using the triangular number trick and the LCM for inclusion–exclusion.

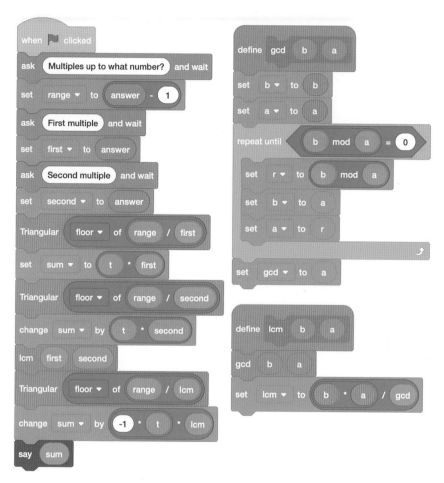

Figure A-59: Summing the multiples of any two numbers

We use a custom lcm block, which first calls our trusty gcd block and then calculates the LCM based on the result.

Challenge 9.3

If the multiples are *a*, *b*, and *c*, first add the multiples of *a*, *b*, and *c* separately, then subtract the multiples of $a \cdot b$, $a \cdot c$, and $b \cdot c$. Finally, add the multiples of $a \cdot b \cdot c$ back in.

Index

Never before has the world relied so heavily on the Internet to stay connected and informed. That makes the Electronic Frontier Foundation's mission—to ensure that technology supports freedom, justice, and innovation for all people—more urgent than ever.

For over 30 years, EFF has fought for tech users through activism, in the courts, and by developing software to overcome obstacles to your privacy, security, and free expression. This dedication empowers all of us through darkness. With your help we can navigate toward a brighter digital future.

LEARN MORE AND JOIN EFF AT EFF.ORG/NO-STARCH-PRESS